A SPANKING GOOD LIFE

D1601507

First Edition

Published by The Nazca Plains Corporation
Las Vegas, Nevada
2011

ISBN: 978-1-61098-295-5
E-book: 978-1-61098-296-2

Published by
The Nazca Plains Corporation ®
4640 Paradise Rd, Suite 141
Las Vegas NV 89109-8000

Cover Photo, Snaptitude
Art Director, Blake Stephens

A SPANKING GOOD LIFE

First Edition

Nick Urzdown

DEDICATION

Taking the decision to write these memoirs was relatively easy, but turning the jumble of memories that tumbled onto the page into legible prose that had a beginning, a middle and an end was a lot harder. It could not have been done without Raven, who blogs at ravenredblog.blogspot.com. She took the trouble to become my unpaid editrix, and without her good humour and patience the disjointed collection of anecdotes that was my first draft would never have been knocked into a shape that could be published. Tony from London also did sterling service with his critiques of the various drafts, and I am grateful to him for that. I ask that both Raven and Tony take what they wish from those parts of the work that they find agreeable, and blame the rest on me.

Nick Urzdown
October 2011

CONTENTS

INTRODUCTION

I was born in 1956 in a country called England, which no longer exists. That country was still racially and culturally homogenous and had certain rules and norms that were taken for granted, and accepted, by the bulk the population.

It was a hierarchical society in which fathers' belts maintained order, helped by teachers' canes and jailers' birch rods. London may have been swinging in the sixties as I grew up, but Manchester was still the socially conservative place it had always been, and that was doubly true of the mill towns that spread out on the city's eastern flank which is the region that I still think of as home.

Spankings were administered by authority figures to those in their charge and this domestic discipline was regarded as normal by all and sundry. Probably my first memory of an actual spanking came during the bitterly cold winter of 1963 when I trudged to a friend's house to see if he wanted to build a snowman with me. As I lifted the knocker on the family's terraced house, I distinctly remember hearing a curious thwacking sound coming from within. As the door was opened I saw the woman of the house standing by the fireplace, holding her bottom through the skirt of her dress, and then I looked to one side and saw her husband threading his thick, black workman's belt back into the loops of his moleskin trousers. I thought nothing of it – I was only seven at the time – and it was only later as my friend and I piled the snow up to build our figure that he told me that his mother had done something or other and that father had given her "a good leathering."

Television programmes of the day reflected this rather casual attitude towards domestic discipline. It would be an exaggeration to say that hardly a week went by without at least one spanking scene being shown on the box, but not all that much of an exaggeration. Western series such as Bonanza and Wagon Train, comedy programmes like I Love Lucy, and drama series typified by the likes of The Saint, all regularly featured a saucy heroine who just needed to be put across the hero's knee to atone for her misdeeds.

My formative years were spent in this background so it is probably not all that surprising that I developed an interest in spanking and began to rather enjoy the thought of putting a girl across my knee and reddening her rump with my hand. Not that I would have avoided correcting a recalcitrant female's behaviour in that manner even though I was not turned on by the act. More than a few people have always regarded a spanking as a purely punitive act and I am sure that I would have joined them in believing that a roasted backside is better than days of sulking and ill-feeling between a couple. Luckily for you, dear reader, I am not like that – or perhaps I am just more honest about what arouses me.

How do I find submissive girls to spank? I do not is the quick answer: I just seek out females and then I spank them. Or rather, I wait until they do something particularly inane – it does not take long, we are talking about women after all – and then I warn them that a repeat performance will earn them a trip across my knee. At that point, madam is more than at liberty to tell me that a smacked bottom is out of the question.

My dealings with the fair sex are governed by the simple rule of *fuck or fuck off*, so if madam decides not to play by my rules then I either throw her out, if we are at my place, or put my coat on and leave, if at hers. If I am going to have to put up with superficial, self-centred prattle about fashion and celebrities then her ladyship had better be very good in bed at the very least. Not only that but she had better not play the prick teaser for more than a day or so, lest I lose interest in her. Probably the only good thing about globalisation is the ready supply of willing females that it has brought to our island's shores, all keen to make their way, often on their backs. The women of Britain really do need to buck their ideas up and take heed of this warning…

Having said that, if madam decides that she wants to carry on seeing me, but doesn't fancy the idea of too many smacked bottoms then all she has to do is keep her innate female silliness under some sort of control and she need never find herself staring at a carpet as her knickers are taken down. I do not invent reasons to spank, and if truth be told what I really want is a quiet life. Needless to say that rarely happens as the natural girlish dottiness always comes to the fore sooner or later, but at least by trying really, really hard the average girl can avoid having her bottom smacked all the time.

My spanking good life was also reasonably remunerative, thanks to some limited talents that I have as a wordsmith. It is said that hard work never hurt anyone, but I have always had my doubts about that idea, and I prefer not to take any chances. As a young man shagging and writing were about the only things that I was both interested in and good at. Alas, nobody seemed interested in paying me as a swordsman, but I did earn a limited number of butties as a puissant scribbler.

If I had to sum up both my views and myself concisely, I would say that spanking to me is a normal, matter of fact way to solve problems in a relationship. It is to my mind closely connected to sex in that I have rarely spanked a woman who is not also my lover. This is about control, and about who wears the trousers in a relationship. The spanking is probably the first part and the sex the second, but they are inherently connected. It has also earned me a bob or two over the years...

Enough of this merry banter! Let us go back through the decades to the very start of the 1970s, to a time when Ted Heath was Prime Minister and Harold Wilson led the Labour opposition. Britain had three television channels and hardly any more radio stations. That was when my spanking life began...

CHAPTER ONE

Early Days

The 1970s were years of growth for me. I was 15 in 1971 when I left school and 23 when the decade ended, so by that time I had been working for some nine years. I drove a car by my late teens, and made the transition from youth to man with a minimum of fuss and a maximum of pleasure. I stood six feet tall, with wavy brown hair that brushed the collar of my shirt in the style of the decade. I was a gangling young man who could fit into a pair of 32 inch jeans, and from the age of 19 I wore a moustache and spectacles. I was never a follower of fashion, being more a jacket and trousers type fellow, but I did make sure that my shoes were always clean, my hair neatly combed and my teeth shining bright. The decade for me was a time of discovery as slowly but surely I came to terms with who I was and what pleased me. What pleased me the most were women, so let us start at the beginning as I retrace my first steps on the road to manhood…

The first spanking

Most of us can remember our first kiss, but I can remember the first spanking that I ever administered as well. Her name was Anita and she was a friend's sister, and the image of her is fixed permanently in my mind as she was the first girl that I ever laid across my knee. We were both 15 at the time, so that puts the date at mid to late 1971. Anita was never my girlfriend as such, but she was one of the first girls that I ever kissed and she would stroke my cock though my trousers. She was also the first girl to ever kiss and gently nibble my neck, something that even today I still find irresistible.

For some reason Anita and I were alone in her house that day. We were chatting about this and that and the conversation took a saucy turn with me teasing Anita about the shortness of her black skirt. I remember asking her if she wasn't worried about the wind catching her nether regions and I hoped that she was wearing thick knickers, it was all very silly and light-hearted.

"Now stop that," said Anita, wagging her finger in that irritating way that women of all ages have. "If you don't I'll have to smack your face for being cheeky."

"If you do I'll take down your knickers for you and smack you somewhere else," I replied.

That was a fairly common thing to say in the England of those days and so was her lightning fast reply:

"It would take a man to do that, not a shirt button!"

So far so normal, but something inspired me to take the matter to its logical conclusion. To this day I am not entirely sure what it was, but I concluded in an instant that the saucy young madam was going to learn her place.

We were sitting in Anita's living room and I left my chair to stride over to her and then sat down next to her on the sofa. I pulled her across my knee and lifted her skirt. She was wearing, and again this image is clear in my mind after all those years, a white crew necked sweater, very thin and with short sleeves that was made of cream lambs' wool. Her skirt was a typical black miniskirt of the day and she wore white knee socks with black shoes that fastened with a buckle to the feet.

She lay quietly across my knee, without moving and nor attempting to cover her bottom. I flipped back her skirt and left it around her waist and for the first time in my life I saw a delightfully rounded female bottom, encased in sweet panties, just waiting for my attention. The panties were white cotton and had light blue lace around the waist and legs. They were not the skimpy variety that girls wear today but high-waisted and designed to give the wearer the illusion of security.

Of course, it was nothing more than an illusion because without pausing for thought I placed the fingers of my right hand into the waistband and peeled them down. There, in front of my eyes, was a bare, defenceless, female bottom just waiting its fate.

Anita tried to put her right hand behind herself to cover her bottom but I took it in my left hand and then administrated three firm smacks to her upturned buttocks. That was all I gave her and then I let her go. She sat up and put her arms around my neck and held me tightly.

"I'm sorry," she whispered into my ear.

That was it. I am sorry to have to tell the reader that there was no sex – I wasn't that bold in those days and at that age – but the incident did teach me a valuable lesson. A girl will often accept a spanking if she feels that she deserves it for some reason. That day in 1971 may have been the first time that I threatened a female with a spanking before going on to administer one, but it wasn't the last. As for Anita, some years later she married a local man and is now a wife, mother and grandmother, but I wonder sometimes if she remembers that far off day in 1971 when I corrected her behaviour in the time-honoured manner?

An outdoor spanking for Julie

I do not know about you but I find an out-of-door spanking rather a pleasant experience. I doubt if many of the recalcitrant females who have found themselves upended in a semi-public spot would go along with that statement, but I am sure that you would agree that it serves them right for behaving badly.

The first time I ever administered an al fresco correction was when I was about twenty. We need to remember that people matured a lot quicker in those days and I had been working for five years by the time I met Julie, who was about the same age as me. As I had just got my first car I celebrated by taking her up to the Pennines that separate the beautiful county of Lancashire from the tribal reserve that sits on the eastern side of the hills.

The spanking has remained in my memory after all these years not just because it was administered outdoors: it also sticks in my mind because it was the first time that I had sex with a girl after having first corrected her.

In other words it taught me that sex and spanking could be intimately related and that the spanking could be used to break down a girl's resistance and make her receptive to the idea of my cock. Ludicrous though it seems to me now, at the time I had never actually made that connection.

I had broken my sexual duck a few months after I dished out my first spanking to Anita, and although I had patted a few rumps and mounted a few mares in the intervening five years the opportunity had never actually arrived to combine the two activities. That is, until the day that Julie went all female on me up in the hills.

We spent most of the early afternoon in a pub before we left and walked up a pathway that started at the side of the building and ran up over the top of a hill. When we got to the top we spent some time sitting on a bench, smoking a cigarette each and admiring the view.

We were not dressed for hiking, and that was what started the silliness. Julie was wearing a grey dress with a broad black belt around the waist and kitten heeled black shoes. The heels may not have been very high, but they were still city shoes, so I objected mildly when she announced that she wished to continue climbing the path that from the point we were at ran steeply up to a much higher hill. I pointed out that the path was narrow, potholed, and very steep, but I might as well have been talking to one of the sheep that were all around us for all the attention she paid me.

She strode off and started her climb, with me following on shaking my head at the foolishness of it all. Sure enough madam slipped and twisted her ankle so I had to pick her up and carry her the hundred yards or so back to the bench. I sat her on my knee and let her complain about the ankle and the state of the path, before eventually and in some exasperation I remarked that none of it would have happened had she listened to me in the first place.

"Now don't be unreasonable, darling," she purred, twisting her ankle from side to side as it recovered from its twist.

"I am not being unreasonable, I am being sensible," was my reply. "Now stay where you are until you recover and we can walk back to the car."

You cannot talk to some women. Julie got to her feet, stuck her tongue out at me, and then started walking off back up the path. I grabbed her arm and pulled her back to the rock.

"Let go of me," she said in a voice that was wilfulness in the extreme. "I can look after myself."

She began to twist and wriggle to free herself from my grasp and then when she realised that this was not going to work she bit my hand, not hard, but enough to cause me to loosen my grip. As soon as I did that she walked off with a look of triumph on her face.

I wasn't going to debate this matter any further. Two steps got me just behind her and I seized her arm and marched her back to the bench. Sitting down I pulled her across my knees and gave her two firm smacks to the rump. Then I pulled the dress up to reveal a firm pair of buttocks nicely clad in dark grey panties that were almost the colour of the dress. Clearly this girl took her appearance seriously, I remember thinking, as I put my fingers into the elastic of the waistband and prepared to lower that final barrier to correction.

The problem was that Julie was kicking and bucking like a wild bronco, and the only way to hold her in position was to cross my right leg over both her thighs and hang on for dear life. Since she had put both hands behind her back to protect her already smarting rump, I had to let go of her knickers so that I could jam her left arm behind me and then hold her right one at an angle in the small of her back. There wasn't time to get the knickers fully down to mid-thigh after that, but I did manage to yank them to just below her bottom. To be honest the struggling was so ferocious that even at the tender age of twenty I knew that if that saucy madam was not corrected immediately she would have broken free and I would have been thoroughly humiliated by my failure.

I gave her about a dozen smacks, alternating one cheek with the other. Each one was well laid on and caused her to yell at the top of her voice as the discipline proceeded. The struggles never abated and I felt that I was losing control of her so having completed a good twelve slaps I pushed her off my knee and onto the ground. It was better to let her think that her spanking had ended because I chose to bring it to a close, rather than give her the victory of breaking free.

Julie sat on the ground and rubbed her bottom with a look of fury on her face. I noticed that tears were about to break out so I sat quietly and smoked another cigarette whilst I waited for her to compose herself. Stubbing out the end of my smoke, I stood up and motioned for Julie to rise. I also noticed, with interest, that the anger had gone from her face and had been replaced by a look of almost helplessness. Her lips quivered slightly, she looked at me with eyes wide open, eyes that were brimming with tears. Although I did not fully realise it at the time, what I had done was to smack all the insolence out of her, leaving Julie with tears as her only defensive option, not through the pain in her bottom, but because of that sense of vulnerability that the spanking had created in her mind. Think about it for a moment, the girl had been stripped of her dignity along with her knickers and had been unable to resist. As far as she was concerned, I had let her off my knee because I had chosen to let her go, not because she was close to escaping.

"Come along, we are going back to town," I instructed her. Julie got to her feet and nodded her head, and then we walked to the car. Neither of us spoke.

Julie was quiet on the way home and kept her eyes down throughout the journey. She sat sideways in her seat and as the journey progressed her hands were drawn more and more to her bottom, to rub and stroke it in the hope of easing the fire that I had lit under her skirt. Again, although I didn't realise it at the time she was obviously mulling over the day's events in her mind and coming to a conclusion about me in the process.

Men really don't think that much about things. If a girl is pretty and has the body shape that we like then we just want to go to bed with her. For the strange, Venusian creatures known as women all sorts of extraneous factors come into play other than the bulges created by a well filled wallet and a long thick penis. What Julie was doing was considering me as a whole man, taking into account all my aspects both plus and minus and weighing me up in her mind to decide if she wished to continue seeing me or not. All of that passed me by given my tender years, but for some reason I guarded my peace as I drove her home and that gave her the space that she needed to reach her decision.

Looking back down the years I think that I had it in my mind at the time that I would drop her off at home and that would be the end of my time with Julie. However, when we reached her house she leaned over and brushed my cheek with her hand before turning to her left to open the car's door.

"Let's go inside," she said, quietly.

The house was empty and as soon as the door closed Julie put her arms around my neck. I held her close and since she kept her head so I turned it up to kiss her. Then I gently stroked her bottom and as she felt my hand on it again her mouth opened to protest and I saw a look of fear flash across her face.

"Don't worry," I reassured her. "So long as you are a good girl your bottom is safe with me."

Julie smiled: "I want to be a good girl," she replied, softly.

We were standing in the hallway and I glanced upstairs and motioned to her that we should climb them. She understood and nodded at me, before leading me to her bedroom.

Once there we undressed each other, then she folded back the bed covers and climbed into bed, to lie there quite submissively until I joined her a moment later.

Lying next to each other I put an arm under her head, and reached down between her thighs with the other one. Julie was wet, and warm, and very, very ready.

"Are you always this available?"

"No," she pouted; as I pushed her onto her back before lifting myself up to mount her.

She exhaled loudly as my cock slid into her body and I began the slow, steady rhythmic thrusts into her.

"I want to be a good girl," Julie whispered in my ear. "Tell me; tell me what you did to me when I was bad. Please, tell me what you did."

So I told her. Quietly, in her ear, as I thrust my hardness into her, I told her how I had spanked her. How I put her over my knee and lifted her skirt, how I had pulled her knickers down and disciplined her. Of course I left out the fact that I only half pulled her panties down and I thought it better to draw a veil over the little matter of only being able to give her a lighter spanking than she deserved because of her kicking, but I don't think that Julie cared about such minor details:

"I was bad, she repeated, over and over again, until eventually she came, followed seconds later by my own shuddering climax.

"But I'm a good girl now!"

Two spankings for Barbara

Sometimes the lessons that I learned were bitter in the extreme and they shame me even today after the passing of so many years. I look back on those times and I shake my head in wonder at my foolishness, and the excuse that I was young and inexperienced in the way of the world rings hollow and false. I just should have known better instinctively: how could I have been so foolish as to hurt Barbara that way when all she wanted was my love?

The lady was a mid-20s sweetie who kept her brown hair cut into an easy to care for pageboy style that was perfect for her hectic life as a student midwife. When we were together in the late 1970s she worked at a Salford hospital, stood about 5' 5" in her stocking feet and was ever so slightly overweight. This was something that troubled her, but it was not a matter that worried me. Partly because I find chubby females rather more of a delight than their scrawnier sisters, but also because bouncy girls tend to have larger bottoms, and when it comes to matters disciplinary that is a decided plus.

I was about to give Barbara a not too serious spanking one evening. We had been playing and she had started to tease me. I took it in good part but warned her that if she did not stop it I would smack her bottom. She had decided to carry on, so I was happily engaged in putting her across my knee and raising her skirt when I detected real fear in her voice as she felt my fingers go into the waistband of her panties.

The struggles became intense and given that she knew that we were only playing I thought this very strange indeed. Barbara twisted her head around and pleaded with me, with genuine fear in her voice, not to take her knickers down. Finding all this very curious indeed I decided to sit her up as I thought that there might be a story worth hearing.

Barbara had been spanked and spanked very soundly indeed, by her father roughly two years earlier. She would have been about 23 when that had happened and clearly her father's action had left a bigger impression on her mind than it had on her bottom. It had not been the first time that he had spanked his daughter, but she had not been over daddy's knee for some years and had begun to think that she was too old for that treatment. Coming home late and answering her father in an insolent manner had taught her the error of her ways. By the time I met her she was not afraid of a spanking per se, but she was terrified of the lowering of the knickers that preceded such a correction.

This was the first time that a spanking tale had been related to me and I questioned Barbara closely about the event. Over the years since then I have invariably asked females if they have ever been taken in hand, and have often been surprised and delighted by the stories that they have told me.

Barbara's father had spanked her in the family home, as her mother bustled around clearing up the plates from the dinner table. Her knickers had been stripped down to below her knees and she had felt her father's hand bounce firmly on her bottom, then down about two hand smacks along to her thigh. That remorseless hand had then returned to her bottom via the other thigh before repeating the process all over again – and again – and again!

Following this account I could not allow Barbara to escape unscathed that night. I put her back across my knee, lifted her knee-length skirt around her waist and hooked my fingers into the waistband of her light blue panties. Barbara moved slightly and began to whimper before putting her right hand behind her to hold her knickers in place. I felt her legs begin to move and realised that I was within seconds of losing control of the situation.

I immediately cocked my right leg over her thighs to hold her in position just as her father had two years before. I then calmly took her left arm and placed it behind my back. Her right wrist was firmly grasped in my left hand and my elbow was jammed into her back just below the shoulders. That young lady was going nowhere until I decided to let go of her.

"Barbara, I decide when you are to be spanked, I decide the severity of the spanking and I decide if you get to keep your panties on or not," I told her calmly.

With that I pealed her panties down to mid-thigh. Barbara let out a cry as she felt that final level of protection being stripped away from her, but other than that she made no sound, nor did she try to break free.

Then I administered the spanking. It was harder than I had intended before she had told me her story, but nowhere near as hard as the correction that her father had administered. Still, I smacked her right cheek, then two smacks on her right thigh, then a couple on the left, before returning to the left cheek and repeating the procedure all over again.

As I held her in my arms afterwards and gently stroked her hair, I reflected that Barbara's father was a man to admire and emulate.

Not that this feeling in any way stopped me from having my way with Barbara shortly afterwards. There is something so delightfully submissive and totally obedient about a newly disciplined female that all my anger instantly dissipates when looking at her. Although Barbara had not been an especially naughty girl that evening I had laid her across my knee and smacked submission into her, and thus she sat next to me, gingerly easing her weight from one bottom cheek to the other, and awaiting my next move like a good girl should.

She didn't have long to wait as I gently cupped her breast through the material of her white blouse and idly circled a nipple so that it became proud and hard even though it was still contained by her bra. Barbara looked up and cocked her head to one side, her mouth slightly open, in the invitation that women have when they want the man to know that they wish to be kissed. I closed my lips over hers and we sank down onto the bed.

Slowly, ever so very slowly, we undressed each other. I kissed her heavy ponderous, yet so very lovely breasts and she reached down and took my hardness in her hand and gently squeezed and stroked it until it reached its full glory.

"What are you smiling at?" I asked her, seeing the enigmatic cast to her lips.

"The way it grows in my hand," she replied, kissing me first on one nipple and then the other.

"Are you moist?"

"I don't know," she answered, coyly. "Why don't you tell me?"

She was moist, and warm and ready as I knew she would be. I pushed her gently onto her back and she instinctively raised her legs at the knees as I climbed on top of her, and then she reached down to take me in her hand and guide me to the gates of heaven.

We made love with a gentleness and slowness that pleased us both and raised our levels of awareness of each other to new heights. We spoke softly to each other, and Barbara stroked my hair throughout our lovemaking, and gently, ever so gently, brushed my neck with butterfly soft kisses, her tongue darting out like a little grasshopper, landing on its target and then quickly scampering away.

Eventually the pace began to quicken. It had to as her tight firm pussy gripped my cock and urged it on to work faster, to pleasure her deeper. Barbara threw her hips forward in time with my thrusts and the tempo built up, faster and faster, until eventually all caution was gone and I was riding her like the wild animal she had suddenly become, onward an onward, faster and faster to our final destination.

"Daddy! Daddy! I am coming, daddy!"

It was the first time that a woman had ever called me by that sweet name, and I felt my balls grow heavy and full and then the muscle relaxed and I could feel my hot rich juices pouring out of me and into Barbara's waiting body.

I am a fool, I know that now. I didn't know it at the time, because I did not fully realise the significance of what Barbara had said to me. To my foolish young ears it was something erotic, but I was unable to grasp the full deep meaning of the word as used by Barbara. She really wanted me to be her daddy and I failed her.

I was not cruel, nor did I cheat on her, but I was thoughtless and nowhere near as caring as she had a right to expect. I led her to believe that I loved her deeply and when she realised that I was just mouthing the words that she wanted to hear, the sense of hurt that she felt was magnified enormously. Eventually we drifted apart and when, about five years later, I realised the full enormity of my own stupidity it was all too late. I made contact with her and took her out to dinner, but the magic had gone. At least I was able to apologise and Barbara was gracious enough to accept the sincerity of my gesture.

Looking back on that affair it eventually taught me the value of honesty with women. They may not like what I tell them – many do not – but they cannot claim that I have ever led them up the garden path. A short while ago I was in the process of breaking up with a married women who had become my mistress, and she had just spent a happy half hour listing all my faults in the self-exculpatory way that women do when they want to justify a decision that has already been made. When she paused for breath I took the moment's silence to tell her quietly that I had never lied to her.

"No, she said softly. "I'll give you that."

The fact that she could agree with my statement is due in no small part to my continuing sense of guilt at my failure to be honest with Barbara all those years ago.

Teaching Sarah to behave

Although I had made the connection between spanking and sex with Julia I had yet to make the full connection between spanking, sex and dominance. That may be hard to believe, but it needs to be remembered that with Julia the decision to go to bed had been hers. I may have contributed to the decision courtesy of my right hand, but she had made the running once we arrived at her home. With Sarah things were very different and the act of control was mine from start to finish, with Sarah in effect merely being along for the ride.

We need to remind ourselves that spanking in the 1970s was difficult in one respect because by the middle of the decade the fashionable girls wore full length evening dresses for their disco inferno nights, something which made their correction that much harder. Trying to lift up a long skirt when the owner is frantically kicking to save her backside from a blistering is not easy and I for one was glad when the styles changed towards the end of the decade and shorter skirts came back into fashion.

I remember taking Sarah, yet another nurse who worked at the Royal Infirmary to what was the hottest disco in town back then. She was a jolly girl with short blonde hair and needless to say that night she wore a full length black gown that left her shoulders bare and which had red inserts in the skirt. She looked quite fetching I must say.

Sarah was a teasing little trollop who enjoyed causing trouble in nightclubs. One of her favourite tricks was to wait until I had gone to get drinks and if I was delayed for any reason then by the time I got back I would find her deep in conversation with some fellow or other. As a rule this game passed me by as I am not the jealous type, but for some reason when she did it that night it irritated me enormously.

I sat down next to her and facing the poor devil that she had suckered in with her female charms as it were. I smiled at him sympathetically – after all none of this was his fault – and then I told him that he was not the first to fall for this trick. I went on, speaking clearly so that Sarah could hear me, to say that he could rest assured as I was going to smack her bottom before she went to bed that night.

He gave me a grin in return and got up from the table. Sarah said nothing, but she fingered the material of her dress in a nervous sort of way. I waited until the drinks had been finished and then I took Sarah's arm, walked her to get our coats and then loaded her into the car for the journey back to the nurses' home.

She hardly spoke during the drive until we were almost in site of the building. Then she found her voice and started complaining that I had no right, no right at all, to give her the spanking that she knew she had coming to her.

"You have no right" she wailed, plucking at the door handle in a foolish attempt to leave the car that was travelling quite fast.

"No right? No right? I've this to give you my right," I promised, pulling my belt free from my trousers and tossing in onto her lap.

She began to get more and more hysterical so I swerved the car into a car park that I knew would be deserted at that time of night. Pulling over in the far corner away from the only entrance and exit I switched off the ignition and opened my door. Before Sarah had time to realise that her moment had arrived I grabbed the belt from out of her hands and yanked her across my knees to leave her body dangling out of the car. Then I used both hands to pull up the skirt of her dress and left it virtually covering her head. I was too angry that night to consider the aesthetics of her bottom, and I just contented myself by peeling her shiny black panties down to her knees.

I folded the belt in two and held it in my right hand. I then lifted my right leg slightly so as to keep her off balance. That way she could not use her hands to protect herself as they were carrying her weight and preventing her face from falling onto the car park's gravel. I placed my left arm over her thighs just to stop her from falling out of the car completely and then I raised the belt above my head and brought it down across her defenceless buttocks as hard as I could.

I gave her a good twenty-five strokes with that belt, each one with the full weight of my arm behind it, and each one raised a good welt on her bare, helpless bottom. By the third or fourth stroke she had started to cry and by the time we had reached a round dozen she was pretty hysterical.

"Please," she whimpered, trying to twist her body to look at me. "I am very sorry."

You will not be surprised to learn that I ignored her pleas and gave her the complete dose, with the full power of my arm behind each one. When it was over I let her rise and she slumped against her door, utterly defeated and without the strength to either lift up her knickers or pull down her dress. Without doubt, she had been taught her place that night.

When the sobbing had subsided she gingerly pulled up her panties and I walked her back to her room, took the key from her hands and opened her door. I pushed her in and unzipped her dress from the back and then I pulled it off her to let it fall to the floor. The bra was swiftly removed and then for the second time that evening her panties came down. However this time the purpose was anything but disciplinary as I laid her face down on the bed, her red, swollen buttocks displayed before my eyes as a mark of my achievement, and then I mounted her doggie-style.

There is nothing more gently submissive and totally helpless than a freshly spanked female, and Sarah had been soundly disciplined indeed that night. Although she didn't say anything, and she hardly moved, I could tell that she wanted to turn to face me. I kneeled up and touched her gently on the left shoulder, Sarah understood immediately and she turned onto her back, wincing slightly as her ravaged buttocks touched the bed. She looked at me imploringly, but did not say a word. Instead she took my hardness in her hand and guided it into her warm, ready body. As I thrust into her she touched my bottom with her hand, pressing down gently on it, imploring me silently not to thrust too hard or too quickly into her.

She had been a very naughty girl indeed, but she had been punished sufficiently, and was back to being the rather lovely girl that I cared for and who occupied a particular space in my life, so we made love just as she wanted, slowly and gently, taking our time, because we had all the time in the world.

Sarah stroked the side of my face with her right hand, her left one she rested on my shoulder. I kissed her eyes as I saw that the tears were starting to form again and she smiled the sweetest of smiles. Slowly, so very, very slowly, we built up the tempo, as my thrusts speeded up and became more demanding. To match this Sarah began to thrust down with her pelvis in time with my movements into her – and so the rhythm built up faster and faster as I felt my balls start to feel heavy and full. Sarah's face rocked from side to side on the pillow, she cried out something unintelligible and raked my back with her nails, then she threw back her head and let out a scream like that of a wounded animal that came from deep within her soul. A second later I joined her and spilled myself into her, as her mouth closed over my right shoulder and her teeth sank into my flesh.

We were spent. We lay in each other's arms, with Sarah idly stroking my hair, neither able to say a word. Eventually I felt obliged to say something, so I uttered the not very original line:

"Behave yourself in future!"

Sarah, smiled sweetly, nodded her head and just to make sure that I understood her true thoughts on the matter, gave me the sauciest wink that I have ever received from anyone.

That is the problem with spankings: they have to be repeated regularly otherwise the lesson is quickly forgotten…

Ending the decade with a whack:
the spanking of Dorothy

Probably the most important single lesson that I took away from my 1970s learning curve was just how normal it is to give a girl a spanking when her conduct warrants it. It is that sense of normality, something that I still have by the way, which makes me roll my eyes when I read some fool writing on the web that he wants a girl to spank. For God's sake, play the man, and find yourself a girl and then spank her when she misbehaves is what I want to scream at those fellows.

Let's take Dorothy as a case in point. Now, I didn't go out with her for very long in late 1979, but I still upended her and she didn't object so I must have been doing something right. She was a primary school teacher who had just been offered a new job in another part of the country, so as we enjoyed each other's company, we both knew that our time together was going to end sooner rather than later.

Dorothy was in her very late 20s in 1979. We were sitting in her house watching television one evening when she became playful, but in an irritating sort of way. Quite how things got out of control has long since faded from memory, but I can remember that she started to throw cushions at me, and then held one up in front of my face to obscure my view of the TV set.

I told her to behave, but she took no notice, so I repeated the instruction with a threat to spank her if she did not do as she was told. As I said that I began to eye her up to see how any correction would have to be administered. She was a small girl, only about five feet tall and wore a dress size ten, so there was unlikely to be much of a battle royal getting her over my knee. The black trousers could have presented a problem but I knew from past experience that they fastened with a simple button and zip combination, so it was really just going to be about standing her up, baring her bottom and putting her in position. I sat back and waited to see if Dorothy would do as she had been bidden, and was not in the least bit surprised to see that she carried on giggling, throwing cushions and generally behaving like a pain.

There was really only one thing to do, wasn't there? I stood up and hauled Dorothy to her feet. Ignoring her protests I undid the button on her trousers and unzipped them. Quickly I spun the wretched girl around so that her back was towards me and I yanked both trousers and panties down to her knees. Spinning her around again I sat down and pulled her across my left knee. My right leg was cocked over both her thighs and her wrists folded into the small of her back. It was the work of less than a minute to get her fully prepared for the spanking that was then about to be delivered.

I did not administer a very sound correction, contenting myself instead with twelve or so firm smacks, given first on one cheek and then the other. Dorothy gasped and whimpered as each one landed with its tell-tale crack across her twitching bottom, but other than that she was lay quietly until I brought the spanking to a close and sat her up on my knee.

She sat there quietly with her head resting on my shoulder. She tried to pull up her knickers and trousers but a firm smack put paid to such silly notions. I unzipped my own trousers, took out my cock, and placed it in her hand. Dorothy stroked it until it became fully hard and then she slid off my lap and onto her knees. Looking deep into my eyes she slowly rubbed my cock in her fist, and then she cast her eyes downward and leant over to take my hardness in her mouth.

There was silence in the room that was broken only by my moans of pleasure. After a few minutes I lifted her head up and gently pushed her back onto the floor. As she guided me into her open body with her hand, she had a smile on her face that lit up the room.

"What's the joke?"

"No joke, it's the carpet rubbing on my bottom," she replied. "It feels funny, that's all."

"What's the matter with your bottom?"

"You know what the matter is," Dorothy said, suddenly becoming very serious. "You gave me a spanking, and my bottom hurts," she concluded, almost in a whisper.

Indeed I had, but that was earlier, and now I was pleasuring both her and myself. The thrusts were long and methodical, and Dorothy squeezed my cock with her pussy muscles every time I pushed into her. Her eyes were hooded and she made low moans in the back of her throat, moans that changed to a scream as her eyes opened wide and her moment of truth arrived.

Afterwards as we lay in that warm after sex glow I looked into her eyes and was rewarded by the sight of her own eyes being cast down. A few moments later a small voice said:

"I am sorry."

There really is not much more that a man can ask for from a freshly spanked female but that she accepts the error of her ways, is there?

Had I been introspective enough to look back on the decade from the vantage point of New Year's Eve, 1979, I would have accepted that my learning curve had been dramatic in the extreme. I had discovered that spanking and sex were closely intertwined and that a woman can be bent to a man's will if he is strong enough to overpower hers. Of course she must want to be overpowered, and I have left out of this narrative the many women who basically told me to take my hook when I threatened them with correction. However, they can be forgotten because what the decade also taught me was that for a reasonably clean, good looking young man, who didn't drink too much and who drove a nice car, well, there was always another girl just around the corner.

I did not have that introspection in those days, what I had instead was a confidence that bordered on hubris which led me to believe that the new decade was going to be my time writ large. That was certainly a mistake as the first two years of it were to prove, but that was for the future. For the present, I not only had the memories of happy times with pretty girls to draw on, but I had also become, quite by chance, a published author. The fact that my publishers tended to be large, thuggish individuals with tattoos up both arms and a tendency to commit acts of extreme violence was not something that I dwelt on. Especially when I was standing in a nightclub with a scotch and dry in one hand and a cigarette in the other, explaining to an impressionable miniskirt about a recent meeting with "my publisher," to discuss "my latest work."

CHAPTER TWO

The 1970s and the Soho Typescripts

I used to think that the tale of a Soho porn merchant who kept a writer in a cellar was apocryphal, but it has been attested to so I suppose that it might be the truth. The story is told that a drunken old hack was given free lodgings in a cellar. At some point in the morning he was woken up, given breakfast and enough booze to keep his hands from trembling, and then he was put to work writing until lunch. After he had been fed he wrote some more until finally he was given a bottle of something or other and could seek oblivion with that until the next day.

The reason why I got involved with the type of characters who keep drunks in cellars was fairly straightforward and had everything to do with my desire for easy money. They say that hard work never hurt anyone, but I have never been one to take chances so going down a coalmine was out of the question. The problem was that heavy manual labour was what most men did so I cast around for something less strenuous and fell into working as a cinema projectionist, a job that I did until I eventually went to university over a decade later. Showing films left me with plenty of free time as the projector was whirring away to do other things, so I looked around for something that I could do in the projection box on the company's time that would bring in money for me.

Looking at the problem from all angles I realised that the only thing that I was even interested in was sex, but I doubted that anyone would pay me for my talents as a swordsman. I was also dubious that the cinema manager would let me install a bed in the corner of the projection box so that a tart could ply her trade with me as her business manager, so to speak. I vaguely toyed with the idea of offering him a cut in the proceeds if he agreed to let an off-duty usherette bang her brains out, but I decided after due reflection that he probably would not be too keen on the idea.

Pondering the matter still further, I began to consider just how many books I read a week to kill time at work. I had always had a love of the written word, so I decided to try my hand at a spot of literary output. I was only twenty and the only thing that I actually had any real experience of was sex, admittedly in industrial quantities, so that meant porn was what I would write. I borrowed a manual typewriter from my uncle and wrote a 5,000 word pornographic short story – all throbbing cocks and gaping vulvas – I am sure that you are familiar with the genre.

The nice thing about working as a projectionist is that I was around Manchester when most decent souls were tucked up in their beds and I had come to know some of the dodgy characters who inhabit any city's hours of darkness. Having completed my epic I went to a particular pub where one of those characters who produced pornography from a printing machine in his kitchen and who I knew slightly was usually to be found and offered him the manuscript. He looked it over and stuck it in his coat. I left the pub with about £3.00 or so in my pocket and my career as a professional writer had begun. Whenever I wanted a spot of extra cash I would knock out a couple of these manuscripts and as a source of easy income, it really could not be beaten.

The only problem was that it was in the merchants' interests to cut out as much of the manuscript as possible, because payment was by the thousand words. Thus if a merchant could cut out the descriptive passages that we writers added to pad out the manuscripts, then he could save himself some money. There was nothing funnier than the sight of some wheezy, chain-smoking, semi-literate, with pencil in hand, trying to edit down a manuscript. Others were more laid back, such as the one who told me in all seriousness:

"If I haven't got a hard-on by the end of the first page, I am not buying this fucking thing!"

What I needed was a niche; something that I could write about effortlessly, and without the need to pad out the pages with superfluous text.

Spanking seemed like the obvious choice, since it was a theme that I was interested in, anyway, and could wax lyrical about. I wrote a story and asked a tame merchant to buy it. His honesty was a joy to behold:

"I don't know shit about the fladge, son, but my punters can't get enough of it. Give me another couple like this and I'll run 'em – what name shall we use for you?

"Call me Nick Urzdown," I replied after ruminating for a moment.

"Is that supposed to be fucking funny, son?"

"Yeah."

"OK, Nick Urzdown it is. I should give a stuff."

I suspect that I may be one of the last writers of Soho Typescripts still alive and kicking, since most of the others were getting on in years when I started back in the mid-1970s. Since I doubt if anyone under the age of about 50 will even know what a Soho Typescript was, I'll explain that back in the day if an organisation needed to get a copy of a document out in large numbers it was done via a duplicating machine, usually called a Gestetner, after one of the companies that made them. The document was typed on an ordinary typewriter, but with a waxed stencil in place of the usual sheet of paper. This stencil was then placed around the duplicator's drum and about 500 copies could be hand-cranked off before a new stencil had to be produced.

An offset-litho printing machine produced large runs just as they do today, and if only two or three copies were needed then carbon paper could be used in the typewriter. However, a run of a couple of hundred copies was usually a job for the Gestetner machine. Needless to say, the Soho porn merchants all bought duplicators between the wars and set themselves up as small publishers. The merchants in other parts of the country quickly copied them, but no matter where the material was produced, it was always called a Soho Typescript.

What usually happened was that a merchant would buy two or three stories of about 5,000 words each from the writers. An artist was paid to produce, on a stencil, the name that was given to the work and a drawing that was vaguely related to it. The connection between the drawing and the content really depended on how much a merchant wanted to pay. I have known some who had a stack of drawings on stencils, which were picked out at random, and then a title written at the top once the merchant had enough stories to justify stencilling them up.

The stories in the typescripts always followed a theme, be it straight sex – always called shaggers in the trade, or fladge – flagellation – which is the trade name for spanking, fem-dom, BDSM and the like. The aficionados and aficionadas may like to say that there is a difference between them, but the trade was far more laid back about such nuances. Thus a certain psychotic Maltese lunatic who ran a large outfit in Liverpool once introduced me to one of his henchmen with the immortal words:

"Meet the bloke who gives me my fladge."

Sadly, within just a few years my career as a writer of typescripts was over. London had already moved away from them and the provinces would follow the capital's lead by the end of the decade. The country had liberalised, and fears of prosecution had eased. Thus it was possible to produce a magazine on an offset-litho machine because a print run of 1,000 copies or so made it economically viable. The legitimate wholesalers were still not willing to carry those titles, but several shops in each provincial city would order up a few dozen copies every month to sell. The second-hand shops, of which there were dozens in every city, would then take the magazines from the customers on a half back deal and sell them on. Those shops also dealt with the local typescript vendors, but as more and more printed works became available the market for the typescripts dried up.

One such professionally printed job was a small magazine called Mentor. In 1971 they produced a spanking special and from that moment on the world of CP fiction was never going to be the same again.

The issue sold out, leading one of the people involved with the magazine to utter the immortal line:

"Every issue has to be a spanking special!"

The magazine only ran as Mentor for a total of four issues, and then had to change its name in a hurry owing to a legal threat from another magazine with the same title. Brainstorming ideas for a new name, someone came up with the idea of the Roman god of the home and hearth, a two-headed being who looks backward and forward at the same time. His name is Janus.

Unusually, and for reasons that are still unclear to this writer, spanking aficionados, rather than the usual collection of drunken hacks who normally oversee a pornographer's output, ran Janus. The owner was a typical Soho hard man, but so long as the magazine was raking it in he was happy to leave the staff to their own devices. The money did roll in as by the mid-1970s, with no real competition around, Janus had a monthly circulation of about 10,000 copies.

It was also cordially loathed by most of the hack writers in Britain. The problem was that Janus had its circle of writers and breaking into that rarefied group was next to impossible – especially for someone from the provinces. The Janus group would sit around and have pseudo philosophical discussions about the meaning of la cosa nostra, which struck me as a faintly silly way to spend an afternoon. The meaning was and is quite simple: we want to make money out of something that gives us a hard-on.

It is pleasant to report that following the death of the editor of Janus, the magazine's writers made an attempt at a coup. An adult film-maker named George Harrison Marks was brought in as a stop-gap editor and he had little interest in the fladge. The writers flounced off to set up a magazine of their own which ran under the name of Phoenix for some years, but it never reached the heights of Janus which seemed to go from strength to strength.

The owner of Janus managed to keep his title, but it was touch and go for a time. Harrison Marks brought out about half a dozen issues of what he called New Janus which he filled with his photographs and whatever unpublished stories were hanging around the office. He was famous for his pornographic films and photographs, but once he realised just how profitable the fladge game was he scampered off to start Kane, his own competitor to Janus, which by then had reverted back to its old name.

Even if all this had not happened Janus was going to face competition sooner or later. The advantage that it had over its rivals had been that most of them were poorly produced, small circulation efforts that paid their writers a pittance. Breaking the Janus monopoly meant that lots of new titles began to appear and for the writers the Golden Age of the 1980s was about to dawn.

As I stood on the cusp of the 1980s life to me seemed to posses an exquisite sweetness. I had a reasonably well-paying job as a cinema projectionist which did not involve a great deal of hard work and which gave me plenty of free time to earn an extra crust with my writings. As cinemas do not tend to open in the mornings, I could have all the late nights I wanted and I became a habitué of the Manchester night life, and the gorgeously svelte females who inhabited that world.

Looking back I approached New Year's Eve 1979 with what can only be described as an extreme case of hubris. As we know, that sense of euphoria is what the gods give men just before they pull the rug out from under them. As I drove to the city centre on the last day of 1979 I had no idea that I was about to come to earth with a resounding crash.

CHAPTER THREE

Eighteen Horrible Months

Looking back, the brief period that ran from January 1980 to July 1981 was for me the best of times and the worst of times. It was a rollercoaster ride that saw me in love twice, dumped twice, and battered from emotional pillar to post by any number of other women to boot. Out of that chrysalis emerged the man that exists today. If you want to understand me as I am now then you need to revisit that time with me. I know that this is a work of erotica, mainly, so I promise to keep the emotional stuff under some sort of control and there will be enough spanking and sex to keep even the most jaded reader content. Nevertheless, in the interests of truth let us take a trip down Memory Lane together…

Joan

The most popular nightspot for Manchester's glitterati in the late 1970s was the Millionaires' Club. Since all the best looking women went there it attracted their hunters in droves, and on New Year's Eve 1979 I was one of those flash jacketed, crisply shirted predators.

Joan was the prey I caught that night, at about 11.30pm, so we saw in the New Year together. This lady was 32 at the time so she was older than me by some eight years. Of Jamaican origin, Joan had lived in the UK for many years and worked as a factory administrator. At around 5' 8" she was tall for a woman and of slender build, but without being too skinny. Her bottom was as firm and rounded as the rest of her, and all in all you can trust me when I say that this lady was truly a delight to bed.

The first time that I placed her across my knee was not long after we had met. We were sitting in her house, being tactile with each other and generally playing in a gentle get to know each other sort of way. Joan said something or other and I jokingly threatened her with a spanking, as I always do with a woman, as a way of judging her reaction to the notion of going across my knee. Joan responded by taunting me which is like a red rag to a bull for a spanking man. I need to point out here that this was all very light-hearted and my intention was nothing more than to remind Joan of just who is in charge that night. So my aim was to put Joan in her place without causing too much injury to her admittedly rather luscious buttocks.

She was wearing a polo shirt and a brown fitted skirt that she had made herself, as she had proudly told me. I put her across my knee and as I lifted up the skirt, to reveal a rump clad in tights with a pair of brown knickers beneath them. I was pulling both garments down when Joan became hysterical and began to plead, as Barbara had some years earlier, to be allowed to keep her knickers on. As with Barbara, I sensed a story and decided to let her sit up so that I could question her further.

Joan had gone out with a white man named Peter from roughly 1976 to about the mid-point in 1979. Like many a woman before her Joan would not tell her man when she was unhappy because she felt that she was being ignored. What she would do was cause trouble to get his attention via an argument. Joan did this to Peter in about 1978 when she swanned off to Chester Races with another man, and then told him about her antics during an argument that she had with him some days later.

According to the story that she related to me, Peter had not argued with her, instead he had undone the button on her jeans and then unzipped the garment. Joan said that she had no idea what he was doing and was even more baffled when he spun her around, placed his fingers inside the jeans on either side of her hips and then yanked them down to her knees with full force. Her knickers quickly went the same way, and then Peter turned her around again to face him, sat down on a chair and pulled her across his knee. By then she understood exactly what was going to happen, but it was too late as his right leg was placed over her thighs to prevent too much kicking and Joan began to receive her first adult spanking.

By her own account she was spanked soundly until she began to cry, at which point Peter let her go, and then waited for her to finish blubbering before he gave her the obligatory lecture as to her future behaviour. The spanking must have done some good because it was over a year until she had to be disciplined again.

The second and final spanking at Peter's hands came in roughly March or April 1979. I am not sure but I think that Joan had again used a trip to Chester Races to get her own back at Peter for some perceived transgression on his part, but even if my memory is at fault with that detail, what is not in doubt is Peter's reaction to the news. That reaction came about as a result of, needless to say, an argument instigated by Joan. She had tossed the news into his face and then ran like the devil up the stairs with Peter in hot pursuit. Joan admitted to me that she knew exactly what he was going to do to her and she realised that she had gone too far this time, hence the flight.

Peter caught her in the bedroom and literally tore the button out of her trousers – Joan's vacuum cleaner found it the next day as she was running it over the carpet. He tore those trousers down to her knees and then her knickers went the same way before she was thrown across his knee. The preliminaries only took a moment before Peter was ready to begin a spanking that Joan remembered only too well a year later when she related the account to me.

He had smacked her first on one cheek and then on the other, alternating the spanks and using all the force of his arm to administer the correction. Joan had tried to struggle but his grip was too firm. She had protested but Peter just ignored her and continued the remorseless spanking. Finally she had broken down in tears which had led to an end to her first spanking but not to this one. Peter spanked on and on and Joan admitted to me that she thought that she had died and gone to hell and that the spanking was her never ending punishment.

"If you ever do that again I will strangle you with your own knickers!" Joan remembered those words with a shudder and went on to relate how Peter then dumped her unceremoniously onto the floor.

He then went for a drive to calm himself down and only returned to the house about an hour later. By her own admission Joan was still in considerable distress, but Peter simply ignored that and stripped off her clothes before taking her to bed. By all accounts it was a knobbing that Joan endured rather than enjoyed, but all in all the events of that night did her the world of good. Certainly, she was still wary of men and the power of their hands when I met her, which made my life a lot easier in those very early days.

Joan had not only been on the receiving end of a couple of well-deserved spankings before I met her, she had also administered at least one as well. That had been dished out to her then husband's lover, and like everything to do with Joan, it was a pretty complicated chain of events that led up to the incident.

Joan and her husband had been in the process of getting a divorce and Joan had moved out of the family home. The husband had met a married woman and was having an affair with her and on the day in question this woman was alone in the husband's house. I cannot remember quite why Joan had to call, but she did and found out that the rumours that the soon to be ex-husband had a lover were true.

The two women began to snap at one another and Joan decided that the matter would be resolved in a corporal manner when she spun her rival around and then bent her over the arm of the sofa. Joan then pulled off her shoe and used it as a slipper to spank the waywardness out of the other woman. I did ask Joan why she had not stripped her rival of her knickers as well as her dignity, and she replied that she had been too angry. The spanking continued until Joan's arm became tired and then she released her victim who promptly scurried out to take refuge in the house of a neighbour.

This is where things became horribly complicated for this writer, because Joan then decided to tell the woman's husband what was going on. However, and here is where I lose the plot, she made it clear that she did not want her husband back. I really cannot get to grips with the thought processes of a person who doesn't want someone, but who decides to cause trouble for them, anyway. I remember when Joan and I were splitting up she asked me what I would do if I ever caught her with another man, and I replied, wearily, that I had little interest in what she did when I was not around.

It should be obvious to any reader that Joan was probably one of the more difficult women who have ever drawn breath. The first real spanking that I gave her came about a month into our relationship. Up until then Joan had been on her best behaviour, fearful that if she didn't mind her manners then she would receive a tanning similar to the one that her ex-boyfriend had given her before she and I had met. However, with a personality like Joan's, such good behaviour had only a brief shelf life as sooner rather than later she was going to revert to her old provocative self.

It was late in the evening and Joan had changed into her nightdress, an ankle-length, cream-coloured nylon affair that was quite transparent. She wore a negligée over it, and on the night in question she had been drinking and was determined to give me grief over something or other. I remember telling her to shut up and that was when things began to spiral out of control.

"I don't want to," came her sullen, petulant reply.

"Try it," I said, keeping my tone as light as possible. Hard though it may be for my reader to believe, but I genuinely didn't want to fight with Joan. I had fallen head over heels in love with her and all I wanted to do was wrap her in my arms and keep the nasty world away from her.

"I said I don't want to," Joan spat at me, taking a deep swig of whatever she had in her glass, vodka tonic I think it was, but I may be mistaken.

"If you don't, then I'm going to have to make you," I told her, my tone hardening so that she could see that I meant it. Actually, I was beginning to feel uneasy. It wasn't that I hadn't smacked a girl's bottom properly before then, but this was Joan, my very special love, and I wasn't sure that I could do it to her.

"Try it, sunshine," said Joan, before rather spoiling the effect with a loud burp.

"One more smart remark and I will."

Joan shrugged contemptuously before trying to put her glass down on the coffee table in front of her, missing and dropping the glass and contents on the carpet.

"I can do what I like and there is nothing that you can do about it, understand, sunshine?"

There was nothing else for it. I had to do something even though I genuinely did not want to. I stood up, yanked Joan to her feet, pulled loose the belt of her negligée, and then pushed the garment off her shoulders and away from her body. Sitting down I pulled Joan across my knee and lifted up the hem of her nightdress to reveal a firm, large, round pair of buttocks neatly encased in brown panties.

I could not afford to mess around this time so the panties came down without any ceremony. Joan's hands were held behind her back leaving her buttocks defenceless and my right thigh was cocked over both her legs to prevent too much kicking. I raised my right hand over my head and prepared to bring it down in a great arc to crash against her newly bared buttocks...

"Stop it," said Joan, quietly, and with a voice that was completely devoid of fear. "I am not playing tonight," she went on in that strange monotone that I had never heard before.

There was nothing else for it: I spanked her very hard. I did not want to and I remember feeling an icy grip in my stomach that was a premonition of something awful on the horizon, but I did it anyway. A good hard, bare bottomed spanking, exactly what Joan deserved that night. And it almost broke my heart to do it.

I remember that I smacked her right cheek rather more than the left, as she was bucking like a wild bronco, and it took all my strength to hold her in position. For those of you who are interested in the technical aspect of a spanking – pretty much all of you I should imagine – in all future spankings I have always managed to alternate the buttock cheeks, but on that occasion one came in for rather more attention than its neighbour.

Joan was spanked and spanked very soundly indeed until she began to cry and then I let her fall to the floor. She lay there blubbering for some time and then looked at me warily through tear stained eyes.

"I am not your child," she said at length.

"Then don't behave as if you are," I told her.

I was expecting another smart remark but she nodded her head in acceptance of my rebuke, and when I held my arms out she sank into them to my intense relief.

Our lovemaking was as gentle as you might expect one of my after-spanking bouts to be. I remember that we lay facing each other in bed, and Joan has a little smile on her lips as she reached down and took my cock in her hands.

"You're making me nice and big, aren't you?"

Joan nodded lazily, and her smile turned into a wide grin as my manhood began to reach its full maturity. I pulled her towards me and kissed her neck, then her breasts, first one then the other, pausing at the nipples to take each one in my mouth, sucking on them greedily until they stood tall and engorged, as sign of Joan's arousal and readiness for what was soon to come.

Soon, but not immediately: Joan had to wait a while yet. I went down between her thighs and my tongue opened her body to flicker within it like the wings of a butterfly. I pushed my tongue into her and fluttered it rapidly up and down before withdrawing slowly and then repeating the action, time and again.

"No, please, please stop," she murmured, as she tried to close her thighs, using all the strength in her legs to bring them together. I pushed them apart with my hands and continued to tongue her, so she arched her back and let out a long, low moan of utter joy.

I mounted her and pushed my cock into her warm, juicy opening. I moved in and out of her body a few times and then I paused, with the tip of my cock just inside the lips of her gaping pussy. Joan threw her hips upwards, but as she did that I pulled back. After a few seconds she looked at me quizzically.

"What do you say?" I asked her, gently moving my cock a half inch or so inside her body and then pulling it out to leave just the tip inside. "What do you say if you're a good girl who wants a poking?"

"Please, please," she whispered, embarrassment written all over her face. "Please fuck me, please do it to me. Please…"

So I did, with deep measured strokes that drove into her body, forcing it open to admit my rock hard cock. Joan began to move her head from side to side, and then she wrapped her arms around my neck and clung on to me like a limpet.

I pushed her back against the mattress and lifted my body up, my hands resting on Joan's shoulders, with my arms as straight as poles. I thrust into her body, my hips moving like a metronome as I fucked her with slow, steady, ponderous strokes that left both of us dripping in sweat as we built up the tempo of my thrusts, with Joan throwing up her hips in time with my downward strokes.

"Bit of the hard, stuff, that's what you're giving me, isn't it? Isn't it? Isn't it?

The speed increased, as I felt my balls grow heavy as the hot juice inside them bubbled to spurt free. I clenched my cock muscles with all my might to try and hold back the deluge, but it was not going to work – I could barely hold back the deluge: the dam was ready to burst.

"I'm coming! I'm coming!" Joan looked at me with a lunatic intensity in her eyes. "Come with me – please come with me," she implored.

So I did. Even if I had wanted to hold back the tide I couldn't have done it. The lock gates inside the canal that ran from my balls to the tip of my cock opened and the hot rich tide of heavy liquid flooded up and rushed along the channel into Joan's eager body.

We lay drowsily in each other's arms and then I reached over to the bedside table and grabbed my cigarettes. I lit one, only for Joan to grab it off me and start to smoke it herself.

"I've stolen your cigarette," she said, as if I did not already know that.

"That's OK," I told her. You stole my heart some time ago."

I would like to report a happy ending to this story but sadly there wasn't one. At least when her previous lover had upended her Joan had behaved herself for quite some time before reverting to her natural feral state, but with me the period of tranquillity lasted only about a month or so. Then it started all over again with another explosion followed by another spanking and then reconciliation again. Then the time between explosions grew shorter and shorter...

To make matters worse, Joan started an almost constant campaign to find my weak spots and then work her way into the emotional hole that she had created to widen the gap until it became a fissure. She stopped confronting me over issues and would back off if I put my foot down, but this was only a tactical manoeuvre, as what she was doing was behaving as a good enemy general should, by exploring my lines and avoiding a direct and costly frontal assault to probe for a weak spot in my defences. Then she would go for that spot with a brutality that still amazes me even today. Once, towards the end, seconds after we had made love, she commented that whatever problems we had, the sex was still rather amazing.

"So I do have something going for me, after all," I said, feeling rather pleased with myself and hoping that things had changed for the better.

"Yes, you should go and be a gigolo," replied Joan, in a voice that had suddenly become toneless, as she cut off that hoped for avenue of escape.

By the very end I was like a losing boxer in the final round of a bout. My eyes were almost closed and I could barely raise my guard to mount the pretence of a defence. I was praying that I could land a knockout blow that would save the situation, but what I got was the final bell and a contemptuous dismissal from the ring.

I was still devastated by the ending of the affair, and it took me perhaps six months to recover and during that time I was a walking disaster area. I met any number of women in a desperate, pathetic attempt to find someone to wrap my arms around and all I discovered was that women can smell the desperation on a loser a mile away. They would use me, get me to act as a free taxi service for them, take them out to expensive places, always with the promise that when we get to know each other better then we can would become closer. Alas, it was nothing but a tactic to keep me hanging around, to take a sadistic pleasure in seeing how far they could dupe me into doing things for them. One little darling persuaded me to let her learn to drive in my car which she promptly crashed and ran off leaving me with a bill for over a thousand pounds.

Eventually I took control of my life and forced myself to calm down and pick up the emotional pieces that were strewn around. By early 1981 I was pretty much back to being my old self, which was a pity, because quite by accident I met Helen, who turned out to be in a class all of her own.

Helen

Helen was yet another one of those nurses that I seemed to bump into in those days. If you are ever in her part of Birmingham you might want to watch out for this one. That said, she was born in 1958, so by now she will almost certainly have passed her fuck-by date. Women just age that much quicker than men, which is probably why they need to move that much faster than us.

Whatever she is like now, back in her day, Helen was five feet nothing of pure sexual delight, a honey-blonde banger who worked at the Manchester Eye Hospital and was 22 when I met her. She had tits like melons, a wobbly bum and blonde hair that looked great spread out all over the pillow. It is true that she did not like swallowing cock oil, but we cannot have everything that we want in this life, can we? She had a lovely little trick of thrusting her hips down and clenching her pussy muscles as a cock was thrust into her. Although you wouldn't believe it to look at her, that girl had ridden many a cock before she came to grips with mine and she was an expert at milking a bull.

To be fair to Helen she accepted spankings as being par for the course for a girl who was a bit on the lippy side. Believe me, when Helen let her mouth run away with her she could be maddening in the extreme. She used to love tormenting her man to see how far she could go before he took her in hand, and was an expert at keeping a fellow at just below boiling point for hours at an end.

Sometimes she would overplay her hand and the thing that I liked about her then was that when she was being placed in the traditional position across a knee she would not plead for a reprieve from her well-earned spanking, rather she would whimper that is should not go on for too long, nor be too hard.

Let me tell you about the most memorable paddling I gave her, memorable because after it was over the night ended with me breaking my duck as far as sex in a car went. Yes, hard though it may be for you to believe, but up to that point I had never rocked a car on its chassis.

A relative of Helen's was due to get married and I drove her to Birmingham for the reception in the evening. Things soured a little bit when I left the motorway and relied on Helen to get me to her family's home in the Great Barr district of the city. Needless to say she got us lost, so I pulled the car over and got the atlas out so that she could direct me using that. When I looked into her eyes all I saw was myself reflected back at me and I realised with a sinking feeling that the little darling could not read a map. When it comes to large breasted females we tend to overlook the fact that their bra sizes are often larger than their IQs, and that was certainly the case with Helen. However, a good pair of bouncers was of no use at that moment so I had to drive and map read at the same time – not a strategy recommended by the way.

"Ever thought about learning basic map reading?" I asked.

"If you're going to be unreasonable with me then I think I prefer to go to this event on my own. All my family will be there and I don't want you being like that."

"Like what? Like the poor sod that has just driven down all the way from Manchester only to get lost because you can't remember where your damned house is? How many Coronation Streets can there be in Birmingham, anyway?

We were a happy pair of bunny rabbits all right and things deteriorated at the reception where Helen insisted upon introducing me to her suburban tribe as a writer with several publications under his belt.

"Are you out of your fucking mind? This lot looks like types who think that sex is what people carry the coal in – how are you going to explain away the fact that I write porno?"

"Babs, please, don't be like that. They don't need to know that," said Helen, blinking both eyes at me.

"Problem is that the fat bloke over there in the cheap suit has read some of my stuff," I said dubiously.

"How do you know that?"

"Well, he asked me what I had written so I gave him some of the titles," I explained, ever the reasonable man. "His eyes sort of lit up when I mentioned *Hot Liverpool Lesbos*, so I promised to sign his copy next time we meet," I concluded in my best conversational manner.

"Did you have to tell him anything?" Helen ran her hand through her flowing locks and fixed me with a stare of pure horror.

"Well it isn't my fault that all they want to do is keep their aspidistras flying, is it?"

The wedding reception from hell ground on to its suitably grisly conclusion, and after saying goodnight to any number of Waynes and Cheryls I managed to load Helen in to the car to drop her off at the family home before returning alone to Manchester.

That was when it all just fell apart. Helen had a bitchy, gritty side to her personality and when it came out she could be an insufferable little madam – and it came out with a vengeance as I drove her home that night. It wasn't exactly what she said, but the way that she said it, in a sullen, resentful, needling monotone that aimed to provoke and which succeeded eventually in its aim.

"Stop it, Kittten, please," I said, using my pet name for her. "Stop it now or I will spank you before this night is over."

"No you won't. I won't let you."

We were driving along a stretch of road in an industrial area. To the left ran row after row of industrial units and to the right a stretch of empty ground ran off into the distance. I pulled the car over to the ground on the right and took Helen firmly by the ear.

"Now listen to me, little girl. I will spank you, I will spank you very hard and I will spank you until you cry, if you don't stop it."

Helen made no reply so I took that as an acceptance and pulled the car back onto the road and continued our journey.

"Take a man to do that," spat Helen.

That was it. There is a limit beyond which a man cannot be provoked and women just have to go over that edge and beyond that limit. Why they do it I have no idea, but Helen did it that night and by God she paid the price across my knee! I swerved the car back onto the waste ground, flung open my door even before the vehicle had stopped properly and yanked Helen across my knee to leave her hanging outside the car with her long hair touching the ground. It was showtime!

I paused for a moment to take stock and looking back I am glad that I did because after all these years the image of Helen across my knee with her firm young buttocks pressing into the seat of her lilac coloured dress is one that has stayed in my mind. Amazingly enough Helen lay in position without a murmur; she made no attempt to struggle nor did she try to cover her bottom. She lay totally submissively in position to await her correction, the only time any woman has ever done that with me.

I used both hands to lift her dress above her waist. Her bottom was clad in the bikini type panties that Helen liked, these being a very pale yellow if memory serves me right. After a second or so to take in the view, I peeled the final layer of protection down and prepared to teach that little girl a lesson that she would remember every time she tried to sit down for the next week.

My right arm was raised above my head and without further ado I brought it down with a crashing smack on Helen's left buttock to leave the perfect imprint of my hard male palm on that soft feminine cheek.

I spanked her soundly, and on alternating cheeks as is my wont, but I didn't hurry the correction along by delivering a flurry of fast slaps. Instead, I spanked Helen methodically, with very sound smacks indeed, each one resounding like a gunshot in the metal confines of my car, and then echoing loudly in the brick canyon of that deserted street.

Throughout the spanking I expected Helen to begin to struggle, to try to protect her bottom with her hand, or to kick her legs in helpless fury, but she did nothing other than remain in position across my lap.

I increased the tempo of my smacks and finally Helen began to move slightly, her hips wriggling noticeably. She still didn't attempt to use her hands in any way, and she still hadn't protested at her treatment, but it was obvious that the correction was starting to have its effect, so I redoubled my efforts as the spanking began to reach its conclusion.

That conclusion arrived a few moments before I intended to stop because Helen dug her nails into my right ankle with all her might and I let go of her. She slumped back against her door and began to howl – she hadn't made a sound up until that moment but she certainly made up for it as soon as I let her go. Out of her lips and from deep within her soul she let out an existential cry of distress that reverberates to this day through the alleyways of my mind.

Helen sat bolt upright in her seat with her legs tucked under her body to carry her weight. The dress was still around her waist and her panties had not been replaced around her hips, but Helen was beyond caring about such sartorial niceties. She cupped her bottom with her hands as if the act of holding it would ease the pain that coursed through both it and her. It was a futile gesture of course, but that didn't stop her trying it, and howling out her anguish in great, gulping sobs. After the antics of the day, she had deserved every smack as far as I was concerned.

I sat quietly like the patient soul that I am and waited for the performance to end. My cock was getting hard inside my trousers, and the thought of what I planned for Helen put a smile to my lips as I lit a cigarette and sat back in my seat to smoke it.

Slowly Helen's sobs turned to sniffles which then petered out altogether. She reached over and took my hand, but I ignored the gesture and took a deep pull on my cigarette, exhaling the smoke through my nostrils. Helen sat by my side, quietly awaiting my next move, or so I thought.

Actually she managed to surprise me. Her silence continued but there seemed to be a curious kind of sucking noise coming from within the car. At first I thought that Helen was sucking on something, but when I looked at her all I saw was her pursed lips and eyes that were suddenly full of devilment. Looking down I saw where the noise was coming from: Helen was gently playing with herself, and the action of her middle finger moving in and out of her warm body was creating the sound.

"Do you like what I am doing?" Helen's voice was liquid soft as she continued to finger herself in the car.

I opened my trousers and pushed them down to my knees. I sat there for a moment watching Helen as she continued her play, her eyes half closed and her mouth slightly open. She rocked her head gently from side to side, and then she looked at me full in the face again.

"Tell me you like it, I am doing this for you," her voice had a catch in it, as if forming the words had suddenly become difficult.

"Christ, I want you," I said, pushing her onto her back and reaching down to grab the handle that would lower the back of her seat. Where the devil was it? Ah! There is was! I pulled it and the seat went down.

"Please, my bottom is very sore," she whispered as I mounted her. She took my cock in her hand and then put her heels onto the edge of the seat so that she could use them to keep her bottom from touching anything. Guided by her hand I pushed my cock into her ready, inviting opening.

"Do it to me," she whispered urgently into my ear. "Give me a seeing to," she went on. "A good one: teach me what's what."

With my arms resting on the top of the seat I trust deeply into Helen's body, the muscles of her pussy contracting just as I started my downward thrust so that my cock had to force her body open to receive the throbbing hardness. Helen then began to rock her hips down in time with each thrust. That combined with the clenching of her pussy muscles was enough to make my balls start to feel heavy with the weight of the hot liquid seed that they contained.

"You spanked me," she said, urgency in her voice. "Didn't mess around did you? I thought that it was never going to stop. The spanking: the spanking you gave me. You spanked me, didn't you? Didn't you?"

Helen's voice took on a great and greater urgency as she relived in her own mind the spanking that I had given her that night. I tried everything that I could think of to keep my balls under control, but the pressure in them had built up to such a pitch that I knew that any moment the gates would open and the surging broth inside them would be free.

All Helen had to do was lick my neck. It was enough to open those gates and my seed pumped into her, filling her body with my hot salty juice

"Yes," said Helen, from deep within her, as her own moment of truth arrived. She pumped her hips up and down to milk the last of my juice, as her nails raked my back. Quite when she put her hands beneath my shirt is still a mystery but the nails dug into my flesh to leave a deep set of lines that she gouged into my flesh with her nails.

We lay in each other's arms with my cock still inside her, albeit rapidly shrinking in size. Eventually Helen's pussy gave out an involuntary couple of twitches, something which it always did and which made me laugh.

"Anyone would think that your pussy was telling me to clear off," I said, drowsily.

"Nobody will ever know it does that, only you," said Helen. I looked into her face and saw the sweetest, most angelic expression there. "Only you, Babs, only you," Helen went on, with a sincerity in her voice that fooled me completely.

She was lying of course, but it was a great performance from a consummate actress. Within a month or so of this event I discovered that the place where I worked was under threat of closure. Foolishly I told Helen that I was probably going to be unemployed by the late autumn, and she went to work finding my replacement with a cynicism that left me stunned.

Helen waited until we had celebrated her 23rd birthday in early July and then she sunk her claws into a certain William, who drove a brand new Range Rover. She quite happily polished two knobs for a couple of weeks, and once she felt that William was truly hooked she gave me my marching orders, three weeks before my own birthday.

To say that I was stunned was putting it mildly. The only bright spot came when William found out what she had done and decided that if it could be done to me then he could quite easily be next in line. So he went along and gave her a final fucking, and then he fucked her off. Other nurses in the medical residence told me that her tears were a joy to behold.

About 1990 I bumped into one of those nurses in central Manchester and she told me that Helen had married some fellow and had two daughters. I remember asking if the husband was father to both girls and my informant answered with a peal of delicious, mocking laughter:

"She did go like a steam engine, I have to admit," she concluded between chuckles.

In the course of my life I have met many prostitutes, but Helen was the only natural born whore that I have ever run across.

New Year's Day 1982 found me greeting the dawn standing on a bridge that runs over the River Irwell. Manchester's then filthy waterway did not have the charm of the Seine or the Tiber, but it did have plenty of balustrades that a weary drunkard could lean against whilst he pondered his next move. Still does as a matter of fact come to think about it.

My car was on one side of the city, my home on another and I was stuck in the middle, still probably unfit to drive and trying to remember the name of the woman with whom I had spent the night. I fished a cigarette out of my pocket and that was when I had my very own epiphany.

Was this all that there was going to be to my life? When not being duped by trollops would I be standing on bridges at dawn wondering where the hell I had been for the past few hours? I had no job and very little money – the writings brought in a little but they never provided me with more than a supplement to a wage that no longer existed. I took a deep pull on my cigarette and as I exhaled the smoke though my nostrils I asked myself the simple question: was I really going to be such a dick in hand loser for the rest of my life?

As the dawn came over the grubby city I saw the way ahead illuminated by it. I would go to university – the fact that I had left school at 15 without a single a qualification to my name was not going to be a problem. I had already done some courses at the University of Manchester's extra-mural department and some more with the Workers' Education Association. They would all help me meet the requirements of the adult matriculation schemes that all the major universities had. In my mind's eye I saw myself as a success, and with success brings with it that hard to define quality of status – and with that comes all the pussy a man can handle!

Needless to say the thought that I might start to climb the corporate career ladder never for a moment crossed my mind. Work to me has always only ever been something that I do for the money so please do not think that

I was suddenly a reformed character. I suppose that I just felt that if I had a degree from an elite institution then a tasty whack would fall into my lap – which funnily enough is pretty much what happened.

All those thoughts were running through my mind as I lit another cigarette and dragged the smoke deep into my lungs before throwing back my head to exhale all the delicious fumes. Of course, if I became a success then I would no longer have to chase women, as they would come after me. Pondering the matter further, I decided to adopt a simple policy that I dubbed *fuck or fuck off* as the basis for all my dealings with the little darlings. If a woman wanted something from me then she had first to be introduced to the bedroom. If I liked the way that she performed, then I might be inclined to pander to her whims. If not, or if she refused my advances then off is where she could fuck, taking care that the door did not bang her arse on the way out of my life. If a woman chose to remain then disobedience would be paid in full across my knee as and when it occurred. Nobody was ever going to be in any doubt who wore the trousers in my relationships.

However, first things first, and I could feel my sense of euphoria begin to grow as I looked ahead to a pleasant few years spending the state's money. Not only were university fees paid in full back in those days, but students received a grant, not a loan. Life for mature students was even sweeter because they received a top-up that would increase my grant almost to the level of the wage that I had so recently forfeited when my cinema closed. So pleased was I by my decision to become a student that I stopped writing my short stories, which was a mistake because it meant that I missed out on the first couple of years or so of the writers' Golden Age which was just around the corner of the new decade.

CHAPTER FOUR

The Golden Age of the 1980s

The very end of the 1970s saw any number of porn merchants trying to get a slice of the Janus pie. Magazines with titles long forgotten appeared, enjoyed a brief spell on the shelves, and then vanished like the early morning dew. However, two factors came together in the very early 1980s to ensure that the old monopoly was going to collapse. The first was the feud that broke out within the Janus organisation that we looked at in chapter two. The second involved the willingness of the wholesalers to carry adult titles.

WH Smith had always refused to stock Janus, but that policy changed in the late 1970s. What that meant was that other publishers could use an already existing distribution system if they could get a title up and running. Until then getting Janus outside London involved a shop buying the magazine each month and waiting for those issues to arrive by parcel post. The change of policy by WH Smith meant that anybody who could guarantee a set number of sales each month could pretty much be sure of their title being carried by Smith's. The London porn merchants hastened to set up their titles.

By the early 1980s Blushes, Kane and Roue were all competing with Janus for the national fladge readership. Many provincial titles also sprang up, most using a more sophisticated version of the old duplicating technology that had produced the typescripts. They circulated in their region and by post to subscribers outside it.

You want to know about money, I can tell. Janus always paid the best, giving its hacks about £25.00 per thousand words. The other titles paid £20.00 and the provincials about £15.00. All of this was cash money, or by a cheque made out to cash, which amounted to the same thing.

By God the money rolled in! Any half decent hack that could stay sober long enough to string a sentence together could be virtually guaranteed a regular income. Janus were their usual snotty selves once they had overcome their little local difficulties, but the other titles took whatever we chose to give them and bloody well liked it. If you do the sums you can see what was going on. Hiring a model, studio and photographer cost a lot of money. Paying me a hundred quid to fill three or four pages in the rag worked out a lot cheaper – and my efforts could be used with stock photos taken from the archives – and that padded out the story to another page at least.

The situation became so ridiculous that I can remember writing a tale called The Master of Blackstone Hall for Roue in about 1988, and being paid £100 for the five thousand word epic. Then I sold the same story to a Sheffield publisher who gave me £75.00 for it. Finally the story was sold yet again for £25.00 to a bloke who ran a spanking newsletter which included a story every month. Sure, I had to agree to change the story slightly and then break it down into five chapters, that then ran one a month in the newsletter, but it was still the same tale at the end of the day.

Of course there were the usual complaints about publishers who "forgot" to pay, but everyone understood the rule that no cheque was ever issued until a writer had complained about its non-appearance. If no complaint was made it was taken that the author in question was basically retarded and such people deserve to be ripped off as a matter of course. To be fair to the publishers of all these titles, none of them really tried to avoid paying their writers – at the end of the day we filled their magazines with product and made their money-spinners into genuine little gold mines.

By the end of the 1980s the hack writers of Britain were a happy bunch of bunny rabbits indeed and then the personal computer arrived and our cups overflowed with both joy and money. The writers discovered that with even a simple word processor package a story could be created and the names, locations and descriptions then added to order to personalise the work. So began the short-lived but highly lucrative trade of personalised manuscripts. The punter would supply the names that he wanted, along with some other details. Half an hour later all that had been added to the already existing story which was then printed up to be posted to the punter next morning.

What could possibly happen to bring an end to this halcyon world? The internet, that's what happened. The trade in magazines just dried up as more and more people joined the computer age in the 1990s. I can remember speaking to a publisher in about 1999 with a view to writing some stories for him and he candidly admitted that the most that he could pay was a tenner per thousand words and he was only offering that for old time's sake and because he knew that I could write. He pulled all his material off the web, an activity that involved hours of plodding through the turgid prose that enthusiastic amateurs had written, but when he eventually found something decent then it could be nicked for free.

I speculated that he must have been rolling in profits and he replied that the glory days were over. Nobody wanted to read magazines any longer, not when they could get everything they wanted on-line. He said that his publication would probably cease that year and sure enough, it did.

Over the first decade of the new millennium all the old titles passed into the history books, but by then I had made a change myself. As I got older I became in demand as an actor in the spanking video industry, about which more will be said in chapter seven.

CHAPTER FIVE

Memories of Oxford and Manchester, 1983-88

Having decided to go to university because of my epiphany on New Year's Day 1982, I spent the rest of that year attending as many extra-mural courses at the University of Manchester as I could so that my university applications would be bolstered by those acts of study. Researching where to go my eye lit upon a small Oxford college called Ruskin, a place that had strong links with the trades' union movement. My union activities would stand me in good stead as part of my application, as would the extra-mural activities. The college asked candidates to research and write a 2,000 word essay from a prescribed list of topics and that I did. I was asked to attend an interview and following that the college made me the offer of a place, so at the start of Michaelmas Term 1983, I loaded the boot of my car up with my belongings and drove down to start my new life as a mature student. To the taxpayers who financed my time within the dreaming spires of Oxford, especially those whose daughters I enjoyed, I would just like to pause here for a moment and say thanks, chaps. Your sacrifices are still appreciated

The anger that had almost consumed me as a result of the 1980-81 hurts had dissipated by the time I reached Oxford, but the lessons had been taken to heart. Never again would I allow any woman to get inside my armour, not that any of them tried at Oxford. We were all students together, all determined to enjoy the magical moments that Oxford provides to every generation that passes through her portals. Is it my imagination or did it never rain during the Trinity Terms that I was around? Did I really spend so many lazy afternoons punting pretty girls along the river and so very many evenings discussing politics in the bar of the Oxford Union?

One thing is not a trick of my memory. Ruskin was a working class college and any Ruskin man who had the wit to get involved in the university societies would be sure of a plentiful supply of bright-eyed, firm-buttocked girls in their late teens and early twenties who were interested in him. Bless their upper middle class hearts, but they loved a bit of rough from time to time and the fact that I had a reputation as a pornographer meant that I was a *bad fellow*, and that factor alone was enough to moisten the panties of many a Home Counties maiden.

So as to better fit in to this new world I grew a beard, an affectation that I kept until late middle age made its colour shift from brown to a salt and pepper hue in 2010, whereupon I shaved it off. I also adopted the Oxford uniform of tweed jackets with corduroy trousers which covered my slightly thicker 35" waist, and for the evenings I invested in black tie since Oxford students love their formal dinners.

It would be nice to report that I then hit the Oxford ground running, but that has never been my style. I did, however, saunter with a bit more gusto than had previously been the case in the direction where the prime pussy was to be found.

Charlotte, the Oxford Cowgirl

The Oxford and County Secretarial College, to give it the full name that nobody ever used, was invariably known as the Ox and Cow and it provided generations of Oxford men with easy pokes. In theory it was all about turning Home Counties *gels* into secretaries, but in practise it was a glorified marriage agency for the terminally thick. As a student in the early 1980s I did my bit to ensure that any Oxford Cowgirl who came within reach of my paws was given a thorough training in the horizontal arts. Not that many of them needed all that much training since they could perform tricks that a Liverpool whore would blush at, but I am sure that you take my point.

Charlotte was one such cowgirl. Just eighteen years old when I knew her, she had long brown hair that fell in delicious waves to the middle of her back, breasts that were eye-poppers and one A-level in English. That latter achievement was the reason why her father agreed to pay the Ox and

Cow's ludicrously high fees because in those days nobody ever thought that the likes of Charlotte even needed to go into higher education, so off they went to become secretaries and husband hunt an executive.

You are not really interested in knowing how we met are you? I thought not – as you can tell I am starting to get to know you – so I will just tell you that it was at a party and the next day we met up for afternoon tea in Browns, of course, and one thing led to another and we ended up at the Eagle and Child in the early evening.

Charlotte kept going on about the Pre-Raphaelites, and at first I just assumed that she had done a half hour art appreciation course at the Ox and Cow, but then I realised that the little darling had dropped a serious clanger as far as I was concerned. She thought that I was a student at the Ruskin School of Art, whereas in fact I was a member of Ruskin College.

Obviously I didn't want to overtax her poor little mind by trying to explain why Oxford has two colleges named after the same fellow, besides I was more interested in getting her knickers down. That I duly did once I had got her back to my room in college with a minimum of fuss and a maximum of squealing. Charlotte's dress soon followed her frillies as did her matching bra – in case you are wondering the set was cream with light blue polka dots; what a good memory I have that I can remember these things after so many years.

Having completed the preliminaries I grabbed a good handful of bouncer and proceeded on my merry way down below. The moment my tongue had parted her labia the little darling let out a yell that I was sure had woken the dead or at least the members of my college which probably amounted to the same thing. Not being a man easily put off his stride I turned my head to the right so that my lips ran parallel with hers, as it were, and then I just let my tongue enter her body before moving it up and down in a side to side motion. I will never forget that she bucked like a bronco and grabbed my hair as if she wanted to prevent me from leaving her pussy lips – as if I wanted to.

Eventually I moved back up above and Charlotte took the opportunity to grab hold of my cock and began to give it a vigorous pulling.

"Careful you don't fire it by accident," I told her.

"What do you mean?" I told you that these girls were not very bright, didn't I? Anyway I explained it all to her and she began to giggle.

"Gosh – me doing that with my hand. Sounds wonderful!"

Clearly the only way to shut Charlotte up was to fuck her, or so I thought, so I climbed into the saddle and began to ride my chosen filly.

As my cock slid easily into Charlotte's body she raised her legs instinctively to take me inside her and wrapped her arms around my neck. She exhaled slowly, her hot breath flowing over my neck and then she sank her teeth into my shoulder. I groaned at the pain but I hoped that she wouldn't stop as it hurt so sweetly. She thrust her hips down in time with each of my strokes, clenching her pussy muscles as she did so. Slowly but surely she increased the speed of her thrusts forcing me to increase my tempo to keep up with her. She stopped biting me and I could look into her face to see an expression of pure joy there, she pursed her lips, and her face took on an intensity that I found delightful.

"Fuck me, fuck me harder," she whispered in my ear, urging me on.

My balls began to get heavy and I could feel that the lock gates that control the canal that runs from them up to the outside were about to open. I had to take control of this girl and the lovemaking otherwise that wonderful evening was going to end before it had properly begun. I grabbed Charlotte's wrists and put them above her head on the pillow, to hold them firmly in my hands. Once she was controlled then I lifted myself up on my arms to give myself a deeper penetration but also so that I could slow down the speed of my thrusts.

"No, no, I want it faster. Can't you go any faster?"

"I do the fucking," I told her. "You get fucked in my time."

"I hate you!"

She rather spoiled the effect of her words by grinning from ear to ear as my cock opened her body up every time it drove deep inside her. She tried to free herself from my grip, first one wrist and then the other, and when that failed she lay back and looked at me with a lascivious intensity. Then she closed her eyes and opened her mouth to let out little cries of the pleasure-pain that woman make when they are being fucked to their intense and total satisfaction.

I increased my speed and at some point I let go of Charlotte's wrists whereupon she immediately threw her arms around my neck and hauled me back on top of her, both our torsos becoming glued together and her arms held me in position. I used my hips the thrust into her and Charlotte used hers to increase the pace of the lovemaking until I lost all sense of anything other than her cries in my ear and the incredible sensation that comes from being between the legs of a lovely teenage girl and having her completely.

It was no use, the pace just had to pick up as urged on by Charlotte I increased the velocity to a killing level. Her head rocked insanely from side to side and she let out a scream that came from deep within her as I felt my balls grow heavy and right at the base of my cock the first lock gate opened to allow the heavy juice that my balls had contained to begin its journey to freedom.

"I can't hold it," I said between gritted teeth.

"Don't hold it, give it to me! Give it to me now! Fill me up with it!"

All my muscles relaxed as if to order. The hot foaming juice shot up and I felt that incredible sensation that is part pain and part release as my juice shot out of me and into Charlotte's gaping, eager body.

We collapsed into each other's arms. There was nothing else to do and nothing that needed to be said. Charlotte wrapped an arm lazily around my neck and we fell asleep like two babes, totally sated by the pleasure that we had given to each other.

Charlotte was the first to wake up as dawn light was filtering into my room. I remember that she kissed me lightly and started to get up.

"I have to go," she said, "we start at nine."

I knew that the Oxford Cowgirls started classes as that unearthly hour so I just nodded. Charlotte got dressed, kissed me goodbye and promised to return later that day. I turned over and went back to sleep as she left the room.

Once the streets had got thoroughly aired I left college and wandered into the Oxford Union for morning coffee and a leisurely read of the newspapers. I stayed there until the bar opened at 11.00am and when it closed again at 3.00pm as all bars did in those days, it seemed a shame to go back to college, so I hung around waiting for afternoon tea to begin. At some point in the late afternoon I finally decided to go back to college to check my pigeon-hole for mail, and I remember strolling through Oxford wondering if I could put off the essay that I had to write until the following morning. I decided that I could as my tutorial wasn't until the afternoon, and with that in mind I decided to go up to my room and read a couple of chapters of one of the books, just to show willing as it were.

I climbed the stairs and opened the door at the top that led to my very short corridor. There, waiting outside my door, was Charlotte, with a face like thunder.

"You shit! You utter and complete shit! You duped me!

"No I didn't," I replied. "What I did was fuck you!" At times like this a laugh and a joke can often diffuse a bad situation, but my little bon mot fell on deaf ears as Charlotte descended upon me, eyes flashing and boobs heaving.

"You lied to me, didn't you, you shit? Go on, admit it," she spat at me.

I must admit that there is something incredibly erotic about a woman on her high horse, the way she breathes in deeply so as to shout more makes her puppies moves sensuously under her clothes. The way that the eyes glitter always reminds me of how they shine when a woman is on her back being fucked, and the mouth that has been opened to complain also opens wide like that to take in a nice juicy cock. Yes, there is something very potent about an angry woman.

Not that a fellow must allow her to go too far out of line, but sometimes it happens and then the filly needs to feel the bit as it brings her back under control. That said, I never expected to have to do that to Charlotte on that day – more fool me for trying to analyse what passes for the thought processes in the female mind.

Charlotte stood in front of me with hands on hips, tapping a foot as she impatiently waited for my answer.

"What do you want me to say?" I was trying as hard as I could to think of anything that could have done that would have set her off in that way, but my mind was a complete blank. For once I was not guilty of the charge, members of the jury.

You said that you belonged to Ruskin College, didn't you? And you lied, didn't you? You're a complete shit!"

"This is Ruskin College," told her patiently.

"No, it isn't!" Charlotte stamped her foot in frustration. "This is somewhere else, somewhere horrid. If this is the Ruskin, where's all the art work?"

Lights suddenly began to come on inside my head. Of course! The silly bitch had confused institutions; I remembered that from the night before.

"You are not in *The* Ruskin, the Ruskin School of Fine Art, but you are *in* Ruskin College. Same man, different aspects of him," I explained, grinning from ear to ear at Charlotte's silliness.

"What? Well, it's still all your fault for not telling me…" Charlotte's voice trailed off as even she realised the idiocy of what she was saying. Not that logic and reason is something that women trouble themselves with over much, especially when they are feeling embarrassed by their latest bout of female silliness.

"Listen, you barmy bitch," I said, sweet reason evident in my tone. "It isn't my fault that you have a bra size larger than your IQ and can't tell the difference between…"

That was as far as I got because Charlotte's hand flashed out of nowhere and cracked across my face! Trust me when I say I couldn't believe what had just happened. Nor could I believe it when I looked up and saw Charlotte's back retreating towards the door at the end of the corridor.

There are times when I am retarded, I really am, and that was one of those times. I stood open mouthed and nursing my smarting cheek as Charlotte exited stiffly towards that door. As she yanked it open, my brain kicked into gear and memories of other women who had strutted out of my life leaving me alone and bewildered flooded into my mind's eye. However, those days had bloody well gone, had they not?

Indeed they had as I demonstrated to myself by sprinting down the corridor and grabbing Charlotte by the neck and then just marching her back to the door of my room. Mine was the last door on the corridor and as we reached it I just pushed Charlotte with all my strength against the wall that ended the corridor and fished my key out of a pocket and quickly opened the door. Then it was a simple matter to almost throw Charlotte inside and slam the door shut behind us. Hands on hips I faced the wretched girl who took a step back a look of pretty total terror on her face as she realised that shit was most definitely about to happen to her.

"Please," she began, lifting her hands in a gesture of supplication. "Please let's talk and…"

That was as far as she got. I just walked the two paces over to her, grabbed her by the neck again, and sat down on the bed, pulling Charlotte over my knee as I did so. She was wearing a blue corduroy A-line skirt that came down to her knees and I gathered the hem in both hands, pulled it right over her waist, and left it dangling over her head. I encircled her waist with my left arm and looked down at the target area that was encased in white cotton panties.

No, I cannot remember exactly what they were like as I was beyond normal anger and had entered a world of utter fury, one where only retribution mattered. Without pausing to lower the panties I raised my right arm and brought it down in the first retributive smack of what was going to be a highly memorable spanking.

To say I gave Charlotte the spanking of her life is putting it mildly. Within a couple of minutes of my first slap landing it had been followed by about fifty more, each one laid on with all the force of my arm behind it. I can dimly remember that I did smack the wretched girl on alternate cheeks, but that was more instinct and experience than a deliberate act on my part. Frankly I was just too angry to think about niceties which is probably why so many of my smacks landed as high as Charlotte's hip bone or as low as her thighs.

To be fair the girl was wriggling like an eel and that always makes perfectly accurate targeting next to impossible. However, my anger was such that I didn't even try to land my smacks in the traditional seat of learning as it were and contented myself with bringing my hand down in a great powerful arc that cracked like a whiplash somewhere near Charlotte's bottom.

Needless to say the recalcitrant young madam was screaming like a scalded cat, but that wasn't what caused me to pause from my labours. What did that was when I became aware at some point that my arm was aching and that was when I realised just how exhausted I was. My heart was pounding in my rib cage and my mouth was open to take in great gulps of air into my lungs.

Charlotte took the opportunity that the respite gave her to try to break free from my grasp. She managed to free her arms from the skirt that had pretty much enveloped them and threw her right hand behind her to cover her bottom.

"No you bloody well don't," I told her as I took the wrist in my left hand and folded it into the small of her back. "I haven't finished with you yet." Weary though I was, the spanking was not over yet as far as I was concerned.

Charlotte turned to her left so that she could look at me with wide tear filled eyes that begged for pity. Alas pity was all used up that day and with a deep breath I looked down at those buttocks that I had been correcting for the previous few minutes and without another thought I hooked my fingers into the waistband and peeled that last line of defence down. Charlotte's bottom was now very red and very bare and the act of lowering her knickers gave her the nudge she needed to open her mouth and let rip another banshee howl of outrage and pain.

My hand was raised again and again it fell in its retributive arc to land on Charlotte's helpless buttock. Now I spanked her methodically, aiming my slaps to cover the buttock cheeks that I had now bared and I smacked on and on until the colour changed from a bright to an angry shade of red.

As the spanking progressed Charlotte's behaviour went from anger, to hysteria, and then to a kind of sullen acceptance. Her struggles didn't cease exactly but they were reduced in intensity and instead of wriggling her hips to escape the force of my retribution she then began to do nothing more than simply twitch her buttock cheeks as each smack landed. I noticed that the arm that I held in my iron grip was not being pulled one way and the other as its owner tried to break it free. The end to those struggles was the proof that all the sauce had been smacked out of Charlotte as all she did was lie across my knee, submissively awaiting my will.

With a final flurry of smacks I dumped her onto the floor where she lay in a foetal huddle, her hands behind her as she nursed her well smacked bottom. I sat quietly for a moment as my breathing returned to normal, and then I got to my feet.

"Listen to me you nasty little bitch," I told her between clenched teeth. "I am off to have a nice long piss and when I get back you will no doubt have fucked off somewhere far away from me."

I actually did more than that. I stood on the roof and smoked a cigarette to give Charlotte all the time she needed to collect her thoughts, pull up her knickers and clear off. However, when I went back to my room after my five minute absence it was to find Charlotte standing by my table. She had obviously pulled up her panties and was leaning against the table on legs that were clearly unsteady. She was shaking and looked at me with eyes that were damp with her tears and filled with uncertainty. That said, there was no insolence left in them, so I was moved to be generous.

"I didn't expect to see you again," I said quietly.

"Just about to leave," Charlotte said, with a hint of sullenness in her voice.

"Do you want a cuddle before you go?"

Charlotte didn't reply; she just held out her arms and as I stepped forward she wrapped them around my neck and began to sob heavily with her face buried in my chest. I held her and waited until the sobs slowly died down and then Charlotte looked up at me. She struggled to find the words, her lips moving silently as she struggled to form them.

"I am sorry," she said eventually, with a quiet sincerity.

I felt all the anger just ebb away in an instant. It was not her words that had that effect on me, because an apology often has no meaning at all. It was her apology and the fact that she stood her ground that made me wrap her in my arms and kiss away her tears. She was proving to me that she was genuinely sorry by her deeds, as well as her words.

I had just demonstrated to Charlotte that women do not get the final word with me, still less the last slap. However, no matter what any woman has done I cannot find it in my heart to continue being angry if she gives me an honest apology and proves the sincerity of her words by her actions in the way that Charlotte did that night. I continued to hold the lovely girl in my arms until her sobs quietly subsided and then we went back to bed.

Charlotte and I had a fling that lasted for some time after the events that I have just described but to be honest I just could not afford to keep her. She wanted to go skiing during the Christmas vacation and I could not afford two weeks in Switzerland, so we drifted apart. Many years later I bumped into her in London as the sleek, well cared for mother of two rather cute children. We had a coffee and chatted about what had happened during the previous decade or so since our Oxford days. At one point Charlotte complained about something that her husband had done so I teased her saying that she should slap him.

"I can't do that," the lovely lady replied. "Look what happened to me the last time!"

Poking in a punt

On the subject of last words and final slaps, one girl who proved that all rules have exceptions was Caroline because she managed to get in the final word herself and turned the slap into a bite, and in telling you her story I have to begin with a simple question: have you ever poked in a punt?

I cannot remember the exact date when I joined that particular club but it was during a delightful Trinity Term when the sun never stopped shining and the girls of Oxford never looked lovelier or more available in their summer finery. I may be getting old, now, but in my mind's eye it is the early 1980s and I was making my way along Cornmarket in the general direction of Folly Bridge with a blanket and a bottle of wine in one hand and a lovely girl named Caroline in the other.

We reached the bridge and I took delivery of one of my college's punts that were moored there. Once bird, booze and blanket were stored away to my satisfaction I took a deep breath and punted us away to one of the tributaries that run off the main river and rammed the punt against a steep bank. The one that I chose had trees running along its top with branches that hung low over the water, in fact some of them actually touched it and I remember having to duck down to get the punt hard against the bank. That done I jammed the punting pole in the mud to leave the craft firmly wedged in place between the pole and the bank and then I turned my attention to other matters.

We drank the wine, and kissed and touched each other, and everything was all very languid and just as it should be on a hot Oxford summer's day. Madam was wearing a light cream dress with roses printed on it and I can remember that it had five large buttons running from top to bottom and a belt that went around her waist. The latter I pulled free and then spent a happy few minutes undoing all the buttons to reveal the prize that lay within.

I suppose that you are expecting to hear a report of her expensive lingerie, so I am sorry to disappoint any underwear fetishist when I state that she was wearing a rather simple but sweet ensemble of matching white bra and panties. The former undid at the front, which made my task a lot easier, and the latter frothy confection of lace and cotton was then pealed down slowly – these things must never ever be rushed – to reveal a sweet pussy, neatly trimmed but not shaven, just as I like them to be.

As I spread the blanket out properly Caroline took the opportunity to sit up and glanced around nervously, holding her long blond hair in a ball atop her head and biting her lip anxiously.

"Are you sure that nobody can see us?" The voice that asked the question was small and uncertain, its owner needing urgent reassurance that everything was well.

"We can't get more private that this," I told her, that being the simple truth. "The trees covered us on the river side and the bank is so high that you would have to stand right on top of it and almost fall in the water to see us. Besides, there's a playing field or something on the other side, and it looks deserted."

That last line was a bit of an invention, very well, actually it was pure tosh, but I didn't think that it would do any harm especially if it calmed the girl down. More fool me, but Caroline sighed and with a final glance around she lay back on the blanket and quietly waited until I had undressed myself and joined her.

So we kissed and touched and she sucked my cock and I stroked her breasts and flanks and we prepared each other as my cock became hard and her pussy grew moist. And everything was just so very right on that long ago day when the sun hung heavy over Oxford and the river waters lapped lazily against the punt as I lay atop Caroline and her hand closed around my cock and guided it into her body.

What more can be said? Caroline was an achingly lovely spring morning of a girl and in all her twenty years I doubt if she could ever have looked as wonderful as she did that day. I looked down at her heavy breasts as they swayed with the rhythm of our lovemaking, and her eyes caught mine and she smiled languidly both with pleasure at the joining of our bodies and delight at the knowledge that I found her so very desirable.

Caroline placed both hands on my face and held it a few inches away from hers, staring deeply onto my eyes the whole time. She clenched her pussy muscles and arched her pelvis downwards in time with my thrusts. I tried to pull away but she clung to me fiercely, looking all the while into my eyes as if she could read my passion for her in them.

I began to build up the speed of my thrusts. As I did so Caroline reached down, twisted somehow to one side and then I felt the fingers of her right hand gently splay across my bottom. I thought that she would rest her hand there to feel my buttock muscles as I thrust deeper and deeper into her body but incredibly she didn't. Instead she inserted her middle finger inside me, not to deep that was impossible, but up to the first joint. Then she moved it in and out in time with my thrusts into her. It was as if I was fucking Caroline as she fucked me and the sensation was exquisite.

"I can't hold it for much longer," I told her, urgency clearly audible in my tone.

Caroline just smiled that lazy smile of hers and slowly nodded her head, her eyes closing as she did so. It was time for both of us.

My muscles relaxed as the great hot surge bubbled up from deep within my balls to spill into Caroline's eager body. She wrapped her arms around my neck as I came and threw back her head to let out a great glorious howl of joy as she felt my cream begin to lap around the entrance to her womb. As I said earlier, everything was just so right on that day…

We collapsed into each other's arms and lay there sated for I can't remember how long. Caroline stroked my hair; a curiously maternal gesture that I found relaxed me even more than I was already. We could have remained like that for an eternity more, but there was sudden splash in the water around the punt. At first I thought that a large fish had jumped out of the water and splashed back into the depths, but then from on top of the bank a small voice piped up:

"May we have our ball back, please sir?"

It just had to happen, didn't it? The playing field was now occupied with small boys all in their bright running around the playing field uniform and they should not have seen us but some budding football star had kicked a ball too hard and it had sailed over everyone's heads to land in the water by our punt. Looking up I saw about half a dozen eager young fellows, all eyes feasting upon Caroline. With a sigh I got up and madam hastily pulled her dress around her, but not before the gang of 11-year olds had finished their impromptu anatomy lesson.

Still buck naked I managed to grab the ball out of the water and somehow tossed it up the six feet of bank where it was taken by one of the spectators. Alas for Caroline they then made no attempt to leave, instead they continued to feast their eyes on her distress and I noticed that grins were beginning to form around several lips.

So did Caroline who clearly was made out of stern stuff. Far from being fazed by this she sat up, holding her dress around her and harangued the merry throng above our heads:

"Haven't you got better things to do with yourselves?" she asked, a silly question if you want my opinion. The fellows obviously felt the same way as none of them moved.

"Want me to come up there and smack bottoms?" I'll do it, you know! You see if I don't! Shorts down for all of you!" That did it – the gang made itself collectively scarce and madam turned her baleful gaze up me.

"You said that nobody could see us didn't you?" Well, what the bloody hell were they? Scotch mist?"

With a weary sense of what was to happen I knew at once that our lovely afternoon was over and a tough evening was about to begin.

As I polled the punt back towards its mooring station underneath Folly Bridge I cursed all nosy children, especially those who liked kicking balls around near me. I remember dreaming that maybe the little bastards who had so ruined my day would end up dead and in the clutches of His Satanic Majesty, and I fervently wished that he would hand them over to one of his more enthusiastic demons for a few millennia of torture. I said something along those lines to Caroline and was pleased to see her take up the refrain:

"Maybe I should phone their headmaster? And get them *caned*," she ruminated, rolling the final word around her tongue with great glee.

"You wouldn't do that – would you?"

"Wouldn't I just! I remember when my brother came home one day nursing six of the best. You should have seen him walking straight legged, it was so funny!" Caroline lay back against her seat and purred like a cat at the memory of happy days of yore.

"Have you ever had to bend over?" I asked, ever the curious soul.

"Nooo, I'm a good girl."

"So nobody has upended you, yet?"

"What do you mean, *yet*? I told you that I'm a good girl."

We carried on with that teasing chatter all the way back to Caroline's college. I must be honest and say that I was relieved that my fears of having another Charlotte on my hands were proving groundless. That said, it did give me a chance to dig around in her past and get some spanking tales. Caroline had been spanked by daddy, of course, and her bottom had felt the hands of two boyfriends, so that was not a bad tally for a 20 year old girl, and the thought of her luscious rump undergoing treatment at my hands fair put a stiffness into my middle leg.

I got my chance soon after we arrived at her set of rooms. I remember sitting down in a comfortable armchair that stood beside the old fireplace and pulling Caroline onto my knee. I idly stroked her bottom as she made herself comfortable on my lap, and as luck would have it madam then decided to climb on her high horse and be a provocative little minx, which was just what I was hoping for.

"I shouldn't have let you in here," she said, scratching her chin and pursing her lips in mock indignation. "You said we were in a private spot and look what you allowed to happen to me. I was so embarrassed... What do you have to say for yourself?"

"Look on the bright side, "I replied. "At least the little scrotes got a free anatomy lesson – ever thought about becoming a teacher?"

"That's a horrible thing to say to me! No, no, take that back at once, those hideous wretches – they saw me!"

I didn't say a word by way of reply, but I did grin widely and nodded my head very, very slowly.

Caroline began the finger pointing routine which is always a good sign from a woman as it means that she is close to having to be being taken down a peg or two. Then Caroline decided to slap me and verily my cup did runneth over.

"Give me your hand," she said, before grabbing my right paw and holding it up for a smack. "I'm going to smack this hand."

"If you do then I will put your across my knee, lift up your dress, take down your knickers and then smack you somewhere else," I told her, trying hard to keep the smile off my lips.

"You just try it," she replied, giving me a glare as she slapped my hand.

Well, a fellow cannot refuse such an invitation, can he? Without further ado I tipped madam across my knee and lifted her dress up to leave it bunched around her waist. I must say that she had looked lovely undressed in the punt, but there is no finer sight to a spanking man that that of a saucy young female helpless across his knee with her panties stretched to bursting point thanks to the delightful orbs within. There is really only one thing to do at such a moment, and that is to peel the panties right down and leave them hanging around their owner's thighs. Just so!

Of course Caroline protested loudly at this treatment but I ignored her protests. What I was unable to ignore was the sight of her lush buttocks that were just waiting for my hand to crack down on them, so as an aperitif as it were I leaned over and ever so gently bit each one in turn.

"Hey," said a female voice from somewhere around the level of my shin, "I didn't know that was how you spanked someone!"

Crack! My palm smacked down across her bottom.

"Is that how they do it?" I asked her in my best innocent tone.

"Er, yes, I think so," she replied, failing to contain her giggles.

Smack! Smack! Smack!

"How about that? Is that a better way of doing it?"

"No, actually I think I prefer the teeth."

"Do you indeed," I said, landing another firm half dozen on her delightful bottom that was now turning a delicious shade of pink.

"Yes, I definitely prefer the teeth, come to think about it."

"Really? But you are a bad girl and bad girls get the palm, don't they?"

Smack! Smack! Smack!

"Yes, they most certainly do and that is what I have just had. But I'm back to being a good girl now, so could you please go back to the teeth?"

You can't win with some women. If she had been a real minx then she would have provoked me into spanking her soundly as Charlotte had recently done, but Caroline knew the weight of a man's balls just by looking at them and she knew just how far to go. I gave her another half dozen to grow on and let go of her. She sat up on my knee and rubbed her bottom ruefully, lips pursed, and face flushed.

"Right, madam," I told her. "It's time for bed!"

So off we went and for the second time that day I got to make love to the lovely Caroline.

Bringing a Hidabeest to heel.

If Caroline took the final word match on points, with Pippa the result was reversed with the trophy being lifted by yours truly, but it was damned close run thing. Far too close for my liking come to think about it.

One of the problems with writing memoirs as opposed to stories is the tiresome need to keep alive some relationship with the truth. Thus, although I have changed most of the names, the narrative concerns events which actually happened and I don't want to tamper with that. So tempting though it is to invent a few outdoor spankings I have actually only ever administered a few such corrections, and only two involved a spot of open air nookie afterwards. The first involved Helen back in 1981, the girl that I wrote about in chapter three, and the second was Pippa, a rather sweet Hidabeest later on that decade.

The Hildabeest has now passed into legend since St. Hilda's College, her natural terrain, has started admitting men. However back in the day standing on Magdalen Bridge and watching the perfumed herd pass by on its way to the grazing grounds and watering holes of Oxford – or expensive restaurants and equally costly bars if you prefer – was a sight to gladden the heart of the most jaded male. After the Oxford Cowgirl the Hildabeest was the commonest prey in Oxford, because like the cowgirl she was relatively easy to catch. Once either or both had been suitably lubricated with cocktails, then the rest of the evening was relatively easy to predict. God knows why St. Hilda's was jocularly referred to as The Virgin Megastore because the idea that any member of the college hadn't wrapped her legs around any number of lusty males was, well, virgin on the ridiculous.

So it came to pass that one evening myself and Pippa the Hildabeest were walking unsteadily along a road late one evening after the bar where we had spent the previous couple of hours had closed. This is England in the 1980s, people, and hostelries closed at 10.30pm except Friday and Saturday when they stayed open an extra 30 minutes. It was March, if memory serves me correctly, and the lady wore a long black overcoat over her undergraduate uniform of wool skirt and blue crew necked sweater. She was also one of the few women who wore glasses, large black-framed things that surprisingly complemented her pretty face which was framed with bubbly blonde hair to perfection.

We were strolling in the general direction of Christ Church, although why we should have done that has long since faced from memory. I do remember suggesting a walk over the bridge and down onto the bank of the River Isis, and that we did before strolling along for a while and then turning off to the left to follow a path that led to a rather nice bench where we sat down to smoke cigarettes.

We started to kiss and Pippa wrapped her arms around my neck and ran her tongue just inside my mouth. I opened her coat and gently stroked one of her breasts and was pleased to see that she arched her back so as to push more of her luscious mound into my hand. Without speaking we got up and as if by telepathic impulse we moved into the trees so that we were sheltered from the path. Not that anyone was around at that time of night but one can never be too careful.

We came to a wooden fence and I leaned Pippa against it and put my arms around her, and I found to my delight that madam was only too pleased to put her arms around my neck and gently nibble my right ear as a good Hildabeest should. She did not object as I put my arms around her rump and lifted her skirt to reveal to my delight that she wasn't wearing thick woollen tights as I had believed but long dark blue socks that reached up to her thighs. Almost as nice as stockings and a damn sight warmer in a chilly Oxford March. I placed the back of my hand over the magical zone that was still covered by her panties and was delighted to find that her heat pulsated onto my hand. That night was going to be easy-peasy I decided. On reflection I should have known even then not to count my chickens until they start going cluckety-cluck.

As far as I was concerned everything was going swimmingly as I inserted my fingers into the elastic of Pippa's knickers with a view to sliding them down over her hips. In fact I may have actually started the peeling down process in train when Pippa froze like a statue, head cocked over to one side, with both hands clamped firmly on my wrists to prevent any further downward movement of her panties.

"Can you hear that?" Her voice was a soft, urgent whisper.

"Hear what?" That's the problem that we fellows have, isn't it? There comes a point in our arousal when the brain switches off and the chopper takes over all necessary processes – and hearing isn't one of them.

"Someone's moving through the underbrush. Listen – the leaves are rustling."

"It's just a rat or something," I replied, and to be fair I had seen out of the corner of my eye a small shape moving around in our vicinity.

"A rat! A dirty big rat! Why didn't you tell me it was a squirrel?

"OK, it's a squirrel," I said, ever eager to both please her and get her knickers down for action.

"Squirrels don't play out at night – it's a dirty big rat and I'm off!" With that madam pushed me away from her and darted back to the path. I shook my head at the inanity of it all and fished a cigarette out of my pocket and stood there smoking whilst a gathered my thought.

"Are you going to stand there all night? I want to go home."

Pippa's voice was petulant and sulky, the tone of a little girl who was used to getting her own way. Alas she had picked the wrong man to play such games with.

"If you want to go home, then see you around," I replied, walking slowly back to the bench where we had sat earlier. "I am quite comfortable here for the time being thank you very much."

"You mean you are going to let me walk on my own?"

"You are not on your own," I told her genially. "You have lots of big fat rats for company."

With a squeal Pippa turned on her heel and started to march off, her heels crunching on the gravel pathway. She turned a corner and was gone from sight but I knew that she had stopped because I could no long hear her footsteps. Knowing that sound travels in the night I placed my tongue into the roof of my mouth and clucked it as loudly as I could two or three times. Sure enough madam returned using high anger to hide her quite entertaining fear.

"I insist that you walk me home," she said, in that attempt at an authoritative tone of voice that women use at times like this: and they wonder why men laugh at them.

"Insist all you like, darling. I leave when I am ready – so sit down and wait," I told her. At that point all Pippa had to do was hang around for a minute until the last of my cigarette had been smoked and then I would have walked her back to the main road and dumped her there. Of course that was too much to ask so she took a deep breath and as soon as I saw that I realised that the remainder of the evening was about to take an interesting turn.

I need to point out at this juncture that I wasn't angry at Pippa, just irritated somewhat by her attitude. It was as if she seemed to think that I should jump to her tune, but since we hadn't had sex at that point I didn't feel any need to be overly enthusiastic about being answerable to her wishes. Not that I would feel all that enthusiastic after sex, either, but I would be more inclined to at least pay lip service to madam and her whims had my knob been nicely shined.

"Now look," she said, wagging her finger under my nose. "You must get me back to my college, safely."

"Sure, when I've finished my smoke, and after I have gone for a walk in the bushes."

"What? What are you talking about?

"I need to go into the bushes to have a pee," I started to explain with all the patience that I could muster, but it was no good because madam was now waving her arms around and then turned her back on me. With a sigh I toddled off into the undergrowth to make some American beer with a view to then taking her home.

"You are a thorough nuisance," I told her after my bladder had emptied.

"Am I? Says who?" I could see to my great pleasure that Pippa's good humour had returned, so maybe the evening wasn't going to be such a waste after all.

"Says me," I told her. "For bringing me down here under false pretences for instance."

"Oooer," Pippa squealed deliciously. "What pretences were those, then?"

"You are all nice and moist, as I discovered when I touched your panties. Got me all hard and ready it did, and then you scampered away. Do you know what we call girls like that in Manchester?"

"No," she said giggling, but of course she did.

"We call 'em prick teasers, and do you know what we do with prick teasers in Manchester?"

Pippa now had a seriously bad fit of the giggles and like most girls in that situation she knew exactly what was coming next, but that didn't stop her shaking her head emphatically.

"We put them across our knees and smack their bare bottoms," I told her.

"If they can't manage it on their own do they get their grannies to help out?" Pippa was almost in hysterics at her sally, but that didn't stop her making a gallop for freedom to escape my grasp. I watched her scamper down the path but brought her to heel with a quick shout:

"Mind the rats – there are some juicy ones on the riverbank!"

Pippa halted dead in her tracks and holding her coat close to her body she began to look all around her on the ground. It really was that easy to reel her in and then all I had to do was walk over to her and grab an arm. Looking back I saw that we were only twenty feet or so away from the bench which would do nicely to sit upon for the matters disciplinary that were to come. I began to walk her back to that place of execution.

"Can't we talk about this?" Pippa enquired, a touch desperately I thought. "I can prove to you that I'm not a tease," she said, brightly. Trust me when I say that Oxford women can think very fast indeed when their bottoms are at stake.

"There is nothing to talk about," I said, trying and failing to hide my grin. We had reached the bench and I quickly pushed Pippa's overcoat off her shoulders and grabbed it as it began to fall to the ground.

"Let's put it there shall we? I said, draping the coat over the back of the bench. Then I sat down and without saying another word I flipped Pippa's long corduroy skirt up and left it bunched at her waist.

With my left hand firmly planted in the small of Pippa's back I took a moment out to feast my eyes on the firm rounded delight that was her bottom. As I write these words the decades fall away and in my mind's eye I can feel her weight on my thighs and the moon is shining down to illuminate her helpless buttocks, clad as they were in a black lace frothy confection that I am sure gave Pippa the illusion of total security. That was until I peeled the garment down to leave her bottom both bare and vulnerable in the chill of that March evening so very long ago.

Pippa gasped as her knickers were lowered, and put her hand instinctively behind her, her legs moving slightly, but other than that she made no move to resist. Clearly this was a lady who had been across a man's knee before, I decided, and who knew that the way to avoid a sound spanking was not to provoke the fellow who was now going to give her a light one. With that thought in mind I raised my right hand above my head and brought it down firmly across the moonlit target below.

"I'm sorry," Pippa whispered. She didn't shout or scream or demand that I let her go. She behaved like an essentially good girl should when she is undergoing a correction and doesn't want it to leave her with a roasted rump. She apologised for her behaviour and relied on me being a decent soul.

Which, dear reader, I hope I am. Obviously I didn't let her go immediately; instead I spanked her soundly giving her perhaps a dozen smacks all told that left Pippa moving sensuously across my lap. She gasped each time my palm smacked her naughty bottom and about half way through the chastisement she apologised again, but other than that she made no sound. To be honest that girl was not an ounce of trouble when undergoing discipline.

With a final lingering look at the bottom that I had just spanked I let Pippa rise and she sat on my knee, brushing her long hair out of her eyes, with a look of complete embarrassment on her face. Then she looked down at the ground, so I lifted her face up to look into her eyes.

"You can rub your bottom if you want to," I told her with a smile.

"Thank you," she said quietly, taking the opportunity to do just that.

"And are you going to be a good girl now?"

Pippa nodded. Good, I thought, as I stood her up and prepared to walk her back into the trees.

I wasn't expecting a struggle and Pippa didn't disappoint me on that score. She leaned against me as we walked into the trees, still with her knickers just below her buttocks. I had my right arm around her waist and her overcoat in my left hand. Believe me; I had plans for that coat...

As we got to the fence where the trouble had started earlier I placed the coat over the top of it and then gently pushed Pippa against the rail so that she would bend over it and be in position for me. I felt her body stiffen as she realised that I planned to have her there and she looked at me pleadingly.

"Do we have to do it here? Can't we go back to my set?"

"Do you want another spanking?"

Pippa shook her head by way of reply and when I pushed her again she bent over the rail, her stomach cushioned by her own overcoat. I lifted up her skirt for the second time that evening and then without ceremony I pulled her panties right down to her ankles and left them there.

Have you ever had a woman that way? There is something incredibly erotic about having her bent over, fully clothed, but with her skirt up and panties down to her ankles. She is ready to receive whatever her man chooses to give her. I licked my right middle finger and began to stroke her pussy with it, all the while undoing my trousers with my other hand. Once they were down and my cock was free I rubbed the head against her moist, gaping pussy and when I was fully hard I mounted her from the rear and began to get a good, steady rhythm going.

She did not shriek or scream, but contenting herself with low heavy moans that seemed to come from deep within her. She reached behind her like a good girl should and took hold of my balls in one of her hands. Cupping them she stroked them with her fingers as I built up the velocity to the killing speed.

It had been quite a night and Pippa was quite a lady. I walked her home afterwards like a good fellow should and as I made my way wearily back to my own college I remember pausing at Carfax, the crossroads that stand in the middle of the city, to light a cigarette. As I stood there quietly smoking I reflected that life really didn't get that much sweeter.

Sadly that was one of my last nights in Oxford as my two fat years in that wondrous place were drawing to their close. I had managed to fool the examiners into thinking that I knew something about history and politics and they had agreed to give me a diploma to prove it. Clutching that I looked around for somewhere else to kill time at the state's expense and the University of Manchester provided me with a cushy berth for the following three years.

Dealing with Bernadette

Bernadette was an achingly lovely girl that I met during my first week at the University of Manchester and who shared a chunk of my life for a couple of years from late 1985. As I look back down the decades, I can say with all honesty that she is the one girl that I still think about with warmth and affection. It wasn't her fault that we split, or mine: we tried our best but it didn't work out and so we sort of drifted apart.

She was 25 back in the summer of 1986, which is when these events occurred. She was a tall, slender, size ten girl, with an infectious smile and a ruddy Irish complexion that she had inherited from both her parents who had hailed from the old sod. She was researching her M.Sc, part-time, at the University of Manchester, worked as a secretary for Marks and Spencer and lived on the top floor of an old house in the south of the city that had been converted into flats.

Although Bernadette was a genuine sweetie, like all females she could be petulant, sulky and generally difficult to handle a lot of the time. She had been across my knee on several occasions and had found the experience less than agreeable. Quite why she was unable to modify her general naughtiness to avoid further correction is something that I am unable to explain, mainly because I cannot get my head that far up my fundament to make sense of many of the things that women do. That aside the spanking that I want to tell you about now was pretty spectacular and even though I am not a gambling man, I would still be willing to bet money that Bernadette will remember it.

Bernadette had been the perfect scatterbrain all that evening. I had called to collect her at the agreed time to find her mooching around in jeans and a T-shirt, having quite forgotten that we were going to the theatre. So of course she needed a bath first but what was she going to do without a pound coin for the water heater? I didn't have one either so a minor drama broke out with Bernadette sat in a chair pondering her next move until I went and got change from a nearby shop. Then she couldn't decide which dress to wear so I had to sit in a chair and be treated to a fashion show as garments were tried on and discarded. Finally she insisted, since this was the theatre and people would look at her, that her admittedly luscious flowing red-brown locks had to be treated to a curling tong whilst still damp. And so it went on… To cut a long story short we arrived in our seats seconds before the curtain went up, Bernadette looking cool and ravishing, with me feeling like a wrung out rag.

We went to dinner afterwards and of course she couldn't decide what she wanted to eat and then went into pout mode when I called the waiter over and ordered for her. Then I was treated to a lecture on how I needed to be more understanding of her whims, and when I told her to shut her pretty little mouth I was told that I was a sexist, which may very well be true, but my agreement should not be used as an excuse to start the sulks all over again.

That was pretty much it for me. I sat back, took a sip of wine and smiled sweetly in Bernadette's direction:

"Have you any idea how hard I am going to smack your bottom when I get you home?"

The couple at the next table overheard my comment, and the woman covered her mouth with a napkin to hide her smile. Her companion and I glanced at each other, with me shrugging my shoulders and him rolling his eyes in sympathy at what I was forced to put up with. Bernadette had more sense than to say a word and the rest of the meal was eaten in silence. Once it was over I paid the bill and loaded her in the car for the drive back to her flat where retribution would follow.

Madam tried to make small talk in the car, but gave up when she realised that I was completely indifferent to her rather desperate attempts to divert my attention from the fact that I intended to take her in hand – and take her in hand pretty damn well – just as soon as we reached her home.

Eventually, but probably far too soon for Bernadette who had begun to pluck nervously at the hem of her silky cream-coloured tea dress, we reached her flat and I pulled the car into the parking area in front of the building.

"Right, young lady," I said to her. "It's showtime!"

As might be expected, Bernadette was in no hurry to leave the car, which was fine because I was in no mood to have a debate with her. I switched off the ignition and climbed out of the car to walk around to the passenger's door. Without further ado I opened it, grabbed Bernadette by the arm, and yanked her out of the vehicle to stand her by my side with her left arm held firmly in my grasp. Then, with her arm pushed upwards in my grasp so that her shoulder was forced up and her whole body was thrown off balance, I started to march her to the door.

"I can walk by myself, thank you very much," she spat, in a quiet voice that was filled with a mixture of fury and helplessness.

"Fine," I replied. "Let's see you do it." I let go of Bernadette's arm and gave her a firm smack to the rump. Trust me she felt that smack through the thin cotton of her dress, at least if the jump she made was anything to go by.

We made it to the front door and Bernadette began to fish in her bag for the house keys. She became flustered and started to grope in the bag, so I just grabbed it from her, got the keys out and opened the door. Then I took hold of madam and pushed her into the hallway.

Bernadette had become not exactly hysterical, but had certainly reached the stage where she was no longer in control of her actions. She cast her eyes around almost in desperation, looking anywhere but straight in front of her where I stood. She hopped from one foot to another, ran her hands through her hair, and then grabbed me by the lapels of my jacket and buried her face in my chest.

"You're frightening me," she said, her voice an octave or so higher than normal.

"You should have thought about all that before you started your antics," was all I said, as I took her hand and led her upstairs.

Bernadette's shoulders drooped as we walked up the two flights of stairs. It was as if she knew that any resistance would be futile and would have only served to earn her a harder spanking – if that were at all possible as my intention was to administer a correction that she would remember every time she tried to sit down for the next week or so.

We made it to her flat, which was basically one very large room in the old house. Bernadette wanted to fuss over things and tried to hang up her bag over the arm of a chair, and reached down to take off her shoes, but I called a quick halt to such time wasting antics and grabbed her by both shoulders, then holding her upright and forcing her to look into my eyes.

"Young lady, you know what is going to happen, and there is really nothing that you can say that I find even interesting at this point," I told her simply. Bernadette gasped and shook her head from side to side. She tried to lift her arms, but I turned, grabbing her by one wrist as I did so, and marched her over to the bed that stood in the other corner of the room. It was high enough for my purposes, and I sat down and pulled the wretched girl across my knee.

"Nooo," she wailed, turning her head to look at me as I placed her left arm behind me back and folded the other one into the small of her back. "Please," she continued a plea that I ignored completely as I flipped up her dress to expose her bottom, fetchingly clad in cream panties that were that trimmed with light blue lace, to my gaze.

Normally I lecture a recalcitrant female once I have taken her panties down, but I knew that Bernadette would burst into tears as soon as that happened. Once she was wailing to the high heavens then I could talk until I was blue in the face for all the good it would do, so in her case the lecture always preceded the lowering of her final defences.

"Now then, little girl," I told her. "I have had a day that I want to forget, but can't, thanks to you and your stupidity. Now I am going to give you an evening that will be just as memorable."

With that I hooked my fingers into the waistband of her panties and calmly, inexorably, I peeled them down to mid-thigh. Bernadette began to cry immediately as I knew she would, but that didn't matter because as I cocked my right leg over her already scissoring thighs, the spanking of the decade was about to begin.

I spanked Bernadette methodically, alternating one cheek with the other, and built up an increasing crescendo of smacks. I cannot remember how many I gave her, but the room resounded to the crack of my palm across her helpless buttocks; buttocks that quickly became first pink, then bright red, before finally turning to the glowing colour of hot coals.

During the whole of her well-earned spanking, Bernadette did nothing but weep bitterly and shake her head from side to side. I could hear over the racket of the spanking that she was trying to form words of protest, but they remained unformed, and all she managed to do was issue strangulated cries as she kicked her legs in helpless frustration.

Finally, with my arm aching and my palm stinging, I brought the spanking to a close with a final flurry of hard smacks, and then I dumped Bernadette onto the floor, to weep to her heart's content. She lay there sobbing for at least five minutes, before finally rising and resting her forearms on my knees.

"Please, she said, piteously, "let me pull my knickers up."

It was a faintly ridiculous request especially since my cock had begun to harden, but I gave her my permission, and she gently reached around behind her and pulled the scanties up, wincing as they covered her ravaged bottom.

Bernadette remained on the floor, with her head down, gently sobbing to herself and stroking her bottom to ease the pain. From time to time she would glance up at me with her big tear soaked eyes, but she didn't speak, contenting herself with the glances. Eventually she moved slightly towards me and reached out towards me with her left hand. She ran it along my legs and rubbed one of my knees, all the while moving uncomfortably from side to side, wincing all the while in discomfort.

"Can I have a hug, please?"

That was all she said and really it was all she needed to say. It was just the little bit of acceptance of her naughtiness that I had been waiting for and I took her in my arms and held her close for what seemed like an age as she continued to sniffle.

Eventually Bernadette looked me full in the face and with the tears fresh on her face; she smiled at me, and cocked her head to one side. She raised her eyebrows and leaned in to kiss me, a long, lingering kiss.

When it was over I stood up taking Bernadette with me. She giggled as she saw my erection jutting out from within my trousers. I unzipped myself and took the throbbing hardness out, to place it in her hand. She stroked me gently as I undressed her. I unzipped her dress from the back and let it fall to the floor. Her brassier was part of a set with the cream panties and that quickly joined the dress. Finally I hooked my fingers into both sides of her panties, and grinned wolfishly at Bernadette as I prepared to lower them:

"It was a waste of time letting you pull them up, wasn't it?" I asked her.

Bernadette squealed in mock outrage and I laughed and picked her up and put her into bed. Stripping off my own clothes I quickly joined her and she put her arms around my neck as I began to nuzzle and kiss her ripe breasts, taking the nipples in my mouth one at a time to harden them with my flickering tongue.

The lovemaking was slow, as it always is with a freshly spanked female. Bernadette kept her arms around my neck as I thrust my cock into her warm, welcoming body. She moved easily in time with me, her body keeping pace with mine as slowly the tempo increased.

At her moment of truth, Bernadette raked her nails deep into my back, drawing blood with them, and throwing back her head to let out the only real noise that she had made during the whole act – a long moan that came from deep within her and which was exhaled at great length. It was a primal cry of pleasure at the end of that joyous act which brought us together again as a couple after what had been for both of us, a pretty horrible day all told.

CHAPTER SIX

A London Interlude, 1988-89

Did I ever tell you that I was a toyboy once? It was 1989 when I fell into the clutches of Rose, who was in her late 40s and the owner of an English language school in London. I was 32 at the time and had signed up to do a Certificate in Further Education at a scratty polytechnic in south London, my reason being that the course, which qualified me to work as a further education lecturer, came with a mandatory, and seriously tasty, grant.

Working for Rose

I was drinking a coffee in a rather nice place just off Jermyn Street the day that I met her. I had noticed the buxom blonde lady of a certain age who sat at a nearby table wearing a rather too severe business suit with one of those 1980s blouses that had a large frilly bow at the neck, as if that feminine touch made up for the rest of the butch ensemble. On the plus side, the high heels were nice and the legs that were encased in sheer black nylon seemed to go right up to the lady's neck. However, viewed from the negative angle she had about her that ice-maiden air that just makes me want to grab any women who have it, yank her over my knee, and teach her not to even think that way around me.

She was looking at me out of the corner of her eye and caught me eyeing up her legs so she decided to treat me to one of those withering glares that foolish women occasionally use on me. I cocked my head to one side and let my tongue out of my mouth before moving it side to side in an obvious sort of muff diving way. To her credit, madam laughed out loud and after that it was plain sailing.

"So, what does a cheeky young fellow like you do for a living?" Madam enquired after I had invited myself over to her table and we had introduced ourselves.

"I'm a student – postgraduate – getting a certificate so I can ride the college lecturers' gravy train."

She laughed at that and asked me some more questions, occasionally crossing and uncrossing her legs, and sitting slightly sideways with her back arched so that her large breasts were made even more obvious. With her head cocked to the side, she fingered the curls in her collar length hair, and every minute or so she would gently touch one of her pearl earrings. She listened intently to my words and laughed at my jokes, her mouth open to show her pearly white teeth. It was quite an expert display and it gave me a serious hard-on in a pretty short order.

With an eyebrow cocked she suddenly reached down into the carrier bag that was at my feet and pulled out the two shirts that I had bought that day. She held them up to consider first one and then the other with her lips pursed.

"Do you buy all your shirts in Jermyn Street?"

"Doesn't everyone?"

"Wear this one on Monday," Rose said, holding a blue and white shirt aloft.

"Where are we going?"

"Nowhere, yet," Rose paused and smiled at me. "I am offering you a teaching post at my English language school, and I want you to look nice."

"To impress the students?"

"Them too."

Thus, an historian who knew nothing about language tuition ended up teaching English to a wealthy collection of Arabs and Latin-Americans for a few hours a week. The rest of the time was spent in bed with Rose, but before that could happen the correct order had to be established. That was done the following Monday when I turned her over my knee and put paid to her incipient nonsense, which was not bad going on our first day together.

Rose's college stood above a shop in central London, and access to it was up a narrow flight of stairs. To say that my first hour or so there was less than auspicious is putting it mildly. Not that I failed to deliver a lesson, rather because I failed to quickly get my hands on Rose who spent the time that I was there strutting purposefully around on her fetishistically high heels, firm buttocks moving sensuously in her fitted, knee-length black skirt as she walked. Given that the skirt had a seriously wide leather belt on it into which a white satin long-sleeved blouse was tucked; the effect she created was authoritative to say the least.

Certainly as far as her minions were concerned she cut an authority figure and she seemed to enjoy sending them off to do her bidding, especially the girls. I noticed that she would often roll her eyes at something a girl said to her before responding brusquely to whatever had been said. With the men she was slightly better behaved, but I suspected that with them she didn't feel the need to climb on her high horse since they were all so pussy-whipped anyway, with their podgy tums, V-necked sweaters and polyester ties. She even tried it on with me, which was a bit saucy, but I just grinned at her before turning my back and returning to my class.

That was what started the trouble because madam waylaid me in the staffroom after the lesson had ended. I was the only one in there as all the classes had ended and the college was rapidly emptying of people. My back was to the door so I did not see Rose come in, but I remember smelling her delicious flowery perfume so I knew who it was and I turned around to greet a face that was trying its best to look thunderous.

"You turned you back on me, earlier on." It was a statement of simple fact, and I merely shrugged by way of reply.

Placing her left hand on her hip, Rose wagged her right index finger in my direction. Her eyes were sparkling, but she somehow managed to keep her lips pursed in a pretence at real annoyance.

"If you do that again, my lad, I'll have to slap your face" she went on, jabbing the blood red nail of that damned finger into my chest to make her point.

"If you do, I will have to bend you over and slap you somewhere else," I told her quietly.

Rose opened her mouth to reply and just at that moment, one of the dickless dwarfs in her employ entered the room and made for the coffee machine. Rose turned to leave immediately, glancing over her shoulder at me as she left the room:

"I will get the book that you need in a few minutes – wait for me outside the flat, please," she said as the door closed behind her swiftly marching frame.

I had no idea what she was talking about and assumed that the mythical book was just a ploy to get me to a flat – but where was that? The college secretary pointed out the door to me as she put on her coat to go home. She went on to explain that a couple of small offices and a bathroom had been turned into a tiny flat which Rose used when she was working late.

As the last of the staff and students left the college, I went through the door and up a very short flight of stairs to a small landing that had three doors leading off it. One was open and led to a tiny bathroom that just about had space for a shower, sink and toilet and the other two doors were firmly shut.

At least that was the case until one opened to reveal Rose standing in the doorway of the very small office that had been refurbished into a sitting room. Looking me straight in the eye she stepped backwards as I walked towards her. She stood in the middle of the room, breathing heavily as I closed the door very firmly and then turned to face her.

I paused for a moment to take in the scene. Behind Rose and against the wall there was a sofa with an armchair next to it, and to my left and against the other wall sat a desk with its chair. I noticed that on the desk were photos of Rose's husband and three children. I would like to report that I felt a twinge of guilt at the sight, but I will not lie: my brain was in the process of switching off and my cock was about to take over. I was distracted by the thought that he was probably off porking his secretary, and then I turned to look in Rose's direction and my cock took over full operational control of my body.

Rose stood in the middle of the tiny room as if rooted to the spot. She held her hands folded in front of her, with her back ramrod straight and her head slightly back. Her mouth was open to show her teeth and her eyes were like slits as they watched me with a passionate intensity. Without a word I took the two strides that brought me directly in front of her and then I idly ran the back of my fingers up and over each of her nipples. As I did so I felt them harden and glancing down I saw that the two delightful mounds were straining against the thin silk of her white brassiere.

"Stop it," she said, heavily.

"No."

"I told you yes," she replied, but making no attempt to stop me.

I turned her around and encircled her waist with my left arm. My right hand continued to explore her heavy breasts and my cock was pressed into her firm, ripe buttocks. I breathed heavily into her neck and she allowed her head to fall backwards so that it rested against my shoulder.

"I am your employer," she breathed quietly.

"Do I look as if I care?"

"You don't, do you? I can tell your sort," she replied, with a hint of desperation in her voice. Then she started to push against me to try and break my hold on her waist.

I had already recognised this madam as a ball breaker of the first order, and I was not going to give her the chance to pull stunts like that on me. I decided there and then that she needed to be brought quickly to heel. All I needed was an excuse and luckily, she gave me just what I needed…

"I could dismiss you for this," she said, defiance now clear in her voice.

"Yes," I told her quietly, my mouth close to her ear. "You could, and maybe you will after what I have finished doing to you."

"What's that?"

"I am going to bend you over and lift up your nice skirt. After I have finished admiring your no doubt expensive panties I am going to pull them down and then I am going to smack your bare bottom until I decide that you know your place!"

Giving Rose time to digest that information would have been counter-productive, so tightening my grip around her waist, I lifted her an inch or so off the ground and then I used my free hand to pull up her skirt as I let her feet drop to the floor. Before she knew what was happening the skirt was around her waist and it was time for act two of the disciplinary drama to begin.

The sofa was no good because it was only a two-seater, so it was not big enough. The armchair had large arms so I would be unable to sit on it and get madam into the traditional position across my knee. Then I realised the answer and without further ado I picked Rose up another inch off the floor again then walked with her like that the two or three paces that brought us behind the chair. I dropped her down and then pushed her body over the back of the chair. She sprawled across the seat, her buttocks nicely upturned, and I placed my left hand firmly into the small of her back to hold her in position. The curtain was about to rise on the final act!

I suppose that I expected Rose to start wriggling and squealing, but she didn't. She moved her body in a half-hearted attempt to break free, but she made no attempt to either speak or put her hands behind her. So I calmly pulled up her skirt to leave her bottom protected only by a delightfully thin layer of white silk, which admittedly covered the target area completely.

"Now then, madam," I announced. "This bottom is going to smart."

With that I raised my arm and brought it down firmly, but not with the full power of my arm behind it, across that lusciously upturned bottom.

"Nooo!" That smack was all Rose needed to galvanize her into action to save her bottom. She desperately flung an arm behind her but all I did was grab the wrist and fold it into the small of her back where I held it out of the way. I then placed my fingers in the waistband of her knickers and stripped them from her buttocks to leave them turned inside out at mid-thigh. Then I raised my hand again and brought it down across the helpless, bare bottom that lay before me.

I spanked Rose soundly, but not cruelly. She had not been naughty, exactly, but she had been a bit on the lippy side, and her incipient insolence needed to be nipped in the bud. Nevertheless, so long as madam kept her protests to reasonable levels and did not act in too provocative a manner, I decided that her bottom would be smacked but not intolerably so. I have my liberal moments, as I am sure that you are aware by now.

The spanking was methodical and by about the fourth or fifth smack I realised that her struggling had ceased and that she was remaining quietly in position, with only a whimper now and then to mark her distress. As I lifted my arm again I decided that it was time to have a short conversation with the wretched woman. To set the stage for that I brought my arm down in a great swinging arc to leave a delightful handprint on her upturned bottom and immediately I opened my mouth to speak.

"Learning your lesson are you, madam?" My tone was conversational, but the edge in it was obvious to any listener. It was up to Rose to respond properly if she wanted this to end soon.

"I am a married woman – stop this!" Rose wriggled her bottom in time with her words but, crucially, she made no move to rise from her position over the back of the chair. I decided that her protests were for show and gave her three or four firm, sound smacks across the bare bottom, a bottom that was quickly turning a rather nice shade of deep pink. I idly wondered to myself if that colour would have to change to an angry and fiery red before the afternoon was out. However, I decided that such speculation was a waste of time and with that in mind I raised my arm again to bring the palm down across buttocks that were then clenched fearfully in anticipation of just such a smack.

"Do you really think that I give a shit about your marriage?"

"I'll tell my husband," she wailed, pathetically. "He'll deal with you!"

"Well, he hasn't done a very good job of dealing with you up to now, has he? Doesn't seem to give a shit what you do, does he?"

I only said those words to have something quick to say, and there was no deep thought behind them, but they seemed to have an immediate effect of Rose. She sighed heavily and her whole body then relaxed. I decided to check her level of submission and I stopped holding her down for the spanking, and contented myself with keeping a proprietarily hand on the small of her back. Rose did not seek to take advantage of that gesture and continued to lie quietly in position as her spanking continued.

Her legs were close together and on impulse I placed the fingers of my hand between them and opened them to leave her pussy open and glistening to my sight. I licked my index finger and slid it into her body and I was delighted to find that she was wet, and slick, and warm. Rose sighed heavily as my finger slid in and out of that inviting pussy and then I saw that she had balled one hand into a fist and had jammed that fist into her mouth, obviously so as not to give me the satisfaction of making her cry out in pleasure.

"Arch your back," I ordered her.

"Why?"

"Because you are a bitch in heat and that is how a bitch stands when she is about to be mounted. Understand?"

With a cry that was part desire and part helplessness, Rose arched her back to receive the cock that would soon be driving into her. Quickly I unbuckled my trousers and let them fall down. My cock sprang free and I stroked it to full hardness with a few slick pulls. Then I placed the head against the opening to Rose's pussy and drove the meat remorselessly inside her. Pulling out I then slowly pistoned it into her a second time to leave it this time deep inside her body for a moment.

"Is this how your husband deals with you?" I asked the question as I began to fuck her methodically with slow steady fuck pokes that had her whimpering as each one was driven deep inside her open, gaping body.

"No," was all she cried.

There was nothing more to say. Taking hold of Rose's hips I levered my cock into her waiting body. Her back remained arched, arched like that of the bitch in heat that she was as slowly, remorselessly, without saying anything further I increased the speed of the fucking.

Rose began to make low moaning sounds from deep within her as her body began to move in time with mine. I looked down at the bottom that I had just reddened and was pleased to see the marks left by my fingers clearly visible on the right cheek. The sight made my cock even harder and my fuck-pace increased dramatically.

I lost control. I could feel the hot juice building up deep inside my balls, Rose was frantically clenching her pussy muscles to grip me harder, forcing me to drive past those muscles, force them to open to admit my cock into her body, a body that was mine, now, mine because I had taken it.

The hot potent spunk bubbled up and flooded out from me and into Rose. She threw back her head as she felt the juices flooding against her cervix, and her cries at the moment of truth for both of us were genuine and wonderful to hear.

Slowly we untangled ourselves and then we both sank gratefully to the floor. Rose rested her head on my shoulder, and she winced as her bottom touched the hard floor. I laughed at that and she looked at me quizzically.

"Is that it?" She stroked my face as she asked the question and for a moment I was puzzled by it. Had it not been enough for her? Rose must have seen my confusion because she spoke again very quietly:

"Will we see each other again or is that it?"

"I was rather hoping that we could see a lot of each other, whenever your husband is not around, I said, giving her a kiss.

Rose purred at my words and snuggled up closer to me.

"We can see each other whenever we want," she said. "Gerald is either at work, playing golf or fast asleep," she added, rather bitterly I thought.

"Excellent news – now then, what about something to eat after all my labours?

"Want me to make you a snack? Let me get dressed and we can go down to the staffroom. I do my cooking there because this place is so small."

"Is there anybody in the college at this time?"

"No, why?"

"Then don't get dressed." Over her protests I stood her up, stripped her of the blouse, bra and stood her out of her skirt and then and sent her off naked with a firm smack to her red rump to make me cheese on toast and a cup of tea.

Give her credit but she got into the swing of things and returned with my snack having put on a large cook's apron that she had found somewhere.

Trust me when I say that there is no finer sight than that of a mature woman, with a freshly smacked bottom on display. Especially when she has brought you some eats and is then sitting there quietly, dressed like a pornographer's idea of a servant, whilst you wolf down your snack.

As I polished off the food I reflected that life probably couldn't get much better. To be honest, what could go wrong with this wonderful new arrangement?

That sense of euphoria known as hubris that the gods give to men just before they pull the rug out from under their feet is a terrible thing and I had it with a vengeance. I pretty much had it made: an income from the government in the form of my student grant, subsidised accommodation in a hall of residence and a cash in hand job from Rose. Not only that but madam provided me with plenty of good sex, and she even ironed my shirts for me. What more could any man want?

As it happened I wanted a lot – everything that London at the very end of the 1980s had to offer, in fact. The Cold War was ending, and the city was already filling up with Eastern European pussy on the make and I made sure that I was first in line to grab some of the primer feline cuts as they became available. The language school did not have any such students, but it was chock-a-block with Latin-Americans and Asians. Rose turned a blind eye to her staff hooking up with students so long as it was done discretely. To be honest most of the male teachers were so pussy whipped that I doubted if they would ever do anything other than scuttle off home to their awfully wedded wives at the end of the day, but there were a couple of likely lads around who looked as if they knew what a penis was for.

For her part Rose knew exactly what my penis was for and she had the full use of it pretty much to order. We kept our affair a closely guarded secret, which meant that hardly any of them men, but almost all the women, knew what was going on.

We would wait until the last person had vacated the building and then scamper upstairs to Rose's little flat. I once worried that her husband just might arrive unexpectedly one day, but she quickly put my mind at rest telling me that he would be at home, tucked up with his hot chocolate in front of the television like a good little boy should.

I suppose that you are after more spanking tales, but truth be told there are none to tell. Rose was an absolute gem both in bed and out of it so I never even had cause to raise my voice to her, still less my hand.

Things could have continued on that merry way into the distant future had not Xochitl from Mexico and Svetlana from Russia both entered my life within days of each other in the early summer of 1989.

From that moment on the shit was just waiting to hit the fan.

Enter Xochitl

For those of you who don't speak Nahuatl, the name Yolaxochitl is pronounced yola-soch-ittle and it means "Flower of the Heart." A girl who carries the name is usually just called Xochitl and that was what I called the red-skinned, lusciously long-haired 20 year old banger who wandered into my life and helped to turn it on its head.

Xochitl turned up in my advanced English conversation class one day, all bright eyed and bushy tailed, wearing Gucci loafers, a pair of jeans that she seemed to have been poured into, and a cream silk blouse that hung outside the jeans and through which her braless shape could be seen. My cock immediately sprang to attention inside my trousers, which is always a good sign that I am taken with a woman, and trust me when I say that Xochitl seriously took me that day.

The six students and I sat in a semi-circle for our class and I tried to concentrate on what they were saying said when all I really wanted to do was grab hold of Xochitl's puppies, then stick my head between them and go brrrrr. I kept some papers on my lap so that my banging great blue-veiner would not be quite so obvious, but Xochitl must have guessed what was going on between my legs because she fixed me with a lazy smile of utter triumph.

As the class ended, Xochitl hung back and I was able to quickly arrange to see her in the coffee shop that stood just around the corner from the college. Over coffee there we agreed to meet the following evening which was a Friday. That was great for me as Rose was never available at weekends since she had to go into loving wife mode, so I immediately had images of being with her from Mondays to Thursdays and Xochitl on Friday to Sunday.

With that in mind I sent Xochitl on her way with a peck on the cheek and a pat on the rump and then headed back to college. Within the hour the place would be empty and Rose would be awaiting her riveting. I decided there and then that the fucking that night was going to be hard and memorable.

The following evening I turned up at the bar where I had arranged to meet Xochitl and sat myself down with a bloody big gin and tonic to wash the taste of students from my mouth and to await the arrival of madam. The appointed hour arrived, and then went, and by a quarter past the appointed hour my glass was empty so I went to the bar and bought another snifter. That in its turn was almost gone when she arrived, looking delightful, I have to admit in a lovely summer dress that was far too bright for an English girl to wear but which looked lovely against Xochitl's lustrous red skin. She sat herself down after having first given me a kiss on the cheek, languidly crossed one leg over another, ran her fingers through the mountain of deep black curls that hung in waves to her shoulders, and then idly fingered one of her large gold hoop earrings.

"I want a drink, please," she said at length.

"What would you like?"

"I don't know. You're the man – you choose."

I wandered over to the bar and got her a vodka and tonic with plenty of ice and another glass for myself. Returning to our table I placed the drinks down and resumed my seat, lighting a cigarette as Xochitl took a long pull on her drink.

"How did you know that this is my favourite? She held her glass up, with lips pursed, and then without further ado she reached over and took my cigarette and smoked it herself.

As I looked into a pair of eyes that sparkled with mischievous delight, I realised that I was about to go into action against an expert player. I did not for a moment believe that vodka was her favourite tipple, and suspected that she would have said that about any drink that I had given her. The trick with the cigarette was hackneyed, but she carried it off very well, and viewed overall Xochitl, gave the impression of being a young women who was experienced enough to be able to judge the weight of a man's balls with just one glance.

That she was after a man who would show her a good time and spend an arm and a leg on her was pretty obvious, and the fact that she had chosen me as her dupe was also as plain as the balls on a dog. The only question that I needed to ponder was whether she would fuck to order in return for the contents of my wallet, or was she a prick-teaser who got turned on by making men yap at her heels like little doggies seeking scraps from her table? I decided that this question needed answering sooner rather than later and Xochitl's late arrival gave me the perfect opportunity to see if she could be brought to heel or just needed to be dumped.

"You arrived late," I started the ball rolling by reminding her of that fact. "Thirty minutes late," I concluded, keeping my voice cold and low.

Xochitl went into girly mode and began to giggle, crossing and uncrossing her legs, all the while twirling her hair in her fingers. She cast her eyes downwards and then looked up at me all the while keeping her head down. Once she saw that I was indeed looking at her she looked away quickly, a nervous smile on her lips. As I said, Xochitl knew how to play a man, and it took all my willpower to avoid ruining things by smiling at her playfulness

"I really don't find anything at all amusing," I said, reaching over to take each of her wrists and hold them down in her lap. As I did that I leaned forward to bring my face closer to hers.

"You little antics have earned you a smacked bottom," I went on remorselessly. I was about to say more when I saw a quizzical look on Xochitl's face.

"I do not understand. Please what does *smacked* mean?"

"I am going to give you a spanking," I told her without further ceremony.

"No, please, no, you can't do that," Xochitl blustered, as I sat back and enjoyed the show. I do not know why she complained quite so much since I had just helped her add another word to her English vocabulary. Given that she was studying for the Cambridge Third Certificate, that was important as I am sure you will agree.

"I can do as I please and you will take what I give you, understand? You want a good time in London? You want extra help with your studies?"

Xochitl nodded her head slowly by way of reply.

"Fine, then do as I tell you," I told her. I might have laid down the law a bit thick, but it is better to clear the air properly where a slapper such as Xochitl is concerned as problems tend to arise if they are given any wriggle room.

We finished our drinks quickly and in silence. Then I stood up and handed Xochitl her bag, gesturing to her with an index finger that she should rise, which she did.

"Right, Pocahontas," I told her. "Let's go back to my place and get this over with!"

The tube trundled its way towards my station with Xochitl fidgeting at my side, her tongue licking her lips constantly, and her fingers playing with the hem of her dress. Occasionally she would try to engage me in chatter, but by and large I ignored her which served to make her even more nervous. I must admit that I do so enjoy it when a naughty girl gets into that state as I just know that her panties are moistening nicely in terrified anticipation of what is to come…

"What was it you called me? Pocahontas? What does it mean?" Xochitl's questions brought me out of my erotic revere, and I half-turned to face her.

"She was an American-Indian princess who married an English colonist in Virginia," I told her.

"An Indian? But I am not an Indian, look at me," she said, jiggling her puppies for effect.

"You have red skin, so you look like an American-Indian," I said.

"Nooo, that is not important. Look, I have short hair; it only comes down to my shoulders. Indian girls have long hair. Mine is nicely curled and Indian girls have theirs as straight as straight can be. Besides, they look like maids, and I don't." Xochitl paused at that point and sat back with a smile on her face as if she had scored a major point.

"Indian or not, you are still going over my knee," I announced.

"Nooooo!"

And so it went on with Xochitl desperately trying to change the subject all the way back to my room in that dreary little polytechnic. It was with a sigh that I opened my door and pushed madam inside. Closing the door behind me I took off my jacket and made a great song and dance about removing a cuff-link and rolling up my right sleeve. I then strode purposefully over to the bed and sat down on it.

I have to be honest and say that I had started to enjoy myself no end. I must admit that the look of a female's face when she knows that a bonfire is about to be lit under her skirt is one to gladden the heart of the most jaded of spanking men. As for me I have never tired of seeing it, and believe me when I say that I was looking at just such a face that night. I lifted up my arm and then pointed to my knee in an unmistakable gesture that she should lower herself over it.

To my amazement Xochitl walked over to me. I could not believe my eyes, as nothing like that had ever happened before. I had placed many a recalcitrant female across my knee and paddled obedience into her, but I had always had to put them into position across my knee and here to my utter delight was a young women walking submissively towards me and then standing so close next to me that her dress brushed against my leg.

I looked up at her face, saw how she bit her lower lip, and then I looked into her eyes to discover that tears were welling up inside them already. A man would have to be an utter shit to take advantage of a woman who was in such a state, and I must confess that I am such a shit, so I grabbed Xochitl's arm and pulled her gently over my knee. As soon as she was in position I lifted up that frothy gold-green dress and left its skirt bunched about madam's waist. Glancing down I was delighted to see a perfectly formed pair of tight buttocks clad in black panties that had what seemed to be knotted strings on either side of them. If I grabbed hold of those strings and tugged, would those knots come undone or were they for show? I decided to find out and was delighted to see that the knots were genuine and once they were undone all I had to do was pull at the back of the panties and the lush red bottom beneath was immediately exposed.

What a sight that bottom was! An absolute delight and such a pretty colour as well. Xochitl may have gone to great lengths to pursue me that she was not actually an American-Indian, but from my point of view she looked like Geronomo's youngest sister. I wondered if it was going to be possible to redden that bottom any more than nature had already left it? Then, with that thought in mind I raised my right arm and brought it down with a solid crack across Xochitl's helpless buttock cheeks.

I spanked her soundly because I wanted her to know that silly female games would not be tolerated, but I would not say that I was cruel to her. After about a dozen smacks well laid on to alternate cheeks I paused my labours for a moment and considered my handiwork. Her bottom had certainly reddened under my ministrations so the fear that a Mexican bottom would not colour under correction was unfounded.

What amazed me though was Xochitl's reaction to having her bottom smacked, or rather, her lack of reaction. She was not trying to be brave – I have experience of that silliness and can usually smack it out of a girl – because she was sobbing quietly. However, she made no move to protect her bottom, nor did she try to escape her punishment. Instead, she lay quietly across my knee awaiting whatever fate in the form of my right hand bestowed upon her.

I was puzzled by this display and I decided there and then that some close questioning of Xochitl was going to be needed later on. However, first things first, as I raised my hand again and delivered a blistering two or three dozen slaps to that delightfully upturned rump and was rewarded by the sight of it gyrating frantically to avoid the hard palm that descended with remorseless efficiency to blister a bottom and to teach its owner the correct way to behave around me.

Xochitl was then allowed to rise, which she did, sitting on my knee with her head resting on my shoulder. She sobbed very quietly without any of the hysterics that women often treat men to when they are freshly spanked and want sympathy for their plight. Xochitl by way of contrast behaved with great dignity, and had accepted my spanking with only the absolute minimum of fuss. As I undressed her for bed I reflected that a man's life would be so much easier if all women could take a leaf from her book.

Xochitl clothed was a delight to view, but naked she was a pornographic fantasy. As the last of the sun's rays shone through my window and onto the bed they reflected off her lustrous skin and made it almost translucent. I sighed with pleasure at the sight and wrapped the lovely lady in my arms and kissed her gently.

I was expecting her to behave in the quiet, submissive way that freshly spanked females often adopt, but she had a surprise in store for me. As our lips met in a gentle kiss she reached down with a hand and cupped my balls. Then, incredibly, her hand began to move underneath my balls and make its way slowly behind me. Her middle finger extended, and I remember my sharp intake of breath as I realised what she planned to do. I arched my back to make it easier for her as that middle finger entered my hole and gently began to lazily turn circles just inside me.

The groan that escaped from my lips was genuine and unforced. I looked into Xochitl's face and saw desire mixed with amusement written all over her features. I smiled back in recognition that she had turned the tables on me rather nicely. Clearly, Xochitl was a girl who was only too happy to take another route if her preferred pathway was blocked. She had tried the coquettish approach and her bottom had paid the price. Now she was about to become my very own courtesan, if I was lucky, so I let my body fall back onto the bed to give her all the room to manoeuvre that she could possibly want.

You may wonder what I was playing at, but I had not gone soft in the head. So long as at the end of the day a woman does as she is told then I am only too happy to let her take control in bed. I am actually rather too liberal for my own good at times because if a woman is very good horizontally then I am usually only too happy to do what she wants vertically. Xochitl had obviously grasped this basic personality flaw in my makeup and was honing in on it with a vengeance.

She took my cock in her mouth and deep-throated me expertly. Her fingers were like butterfly wings on my balls and then I felt that magic middle finger insert itself inside my once again – and this time it went right in!

Xochitl sucked my cock and finger fucked me all the way to glory. I remember feeling my juices beginning to bubble and for a second I was tempted to push her onto her back, pause a moment to let the raging torrent subside, and then rivet her rigidly, but then I decided not to bother. As the *fuck it* principle kicked in I felt my cock muscles relax and the boiling juices began that remorseless rise through my cock and out into Xochitl's eager mouth. I grabbed her hair at the very moment of truth and held her head over my hardness so that she would continue sucking out every last drop of my cock oil.

"Will you take me to a nightclub?" The voice was chirpy and so full of life that I could not help but laugh. Of course I would, later…

I was still a little curious to know why Xochitl had zeroed in on me, so I took the opportunity that the rest provided to ask some roundabout questions. The answer lay in her background. Xochitl's mother had been very poor and had managed to hustle her way into a job as a secretary that had, fortuitously, brought her into contact with a seriously wealthy businessman who had made her his permanent mistress. In the fullness of time Xochitl had arrived on the scene and the father had ensured that she received a good education in schools that were as far away from his legitimate family as it was possible to get. Every year daddy packed her off to London for a couple of months to study English, so all madam was doing was putting into practise with me the techniques that she had learned from her mother. I must say it is nice to hear of a mother passing her trade skills down to her daughter…

In addition, yes, daddy did spank her when she was naughty, as he did her mother as well. So that accounted for the way that she had positioned herself across my knee. It is so nice to have one's suspicions confirmed.

That aside, it was obvious that Xochitl was going to be an expensive hobby, which was the reason why I ended up running a Russian whore named Svetlana around the city, and indirectly why everything fell apart, but that was in the future. For the moment I felt like a dog with two dicks as I serviced Rose and Xochitl, depending upon what day of the week it was.

It saddens me to have to relate that Xochitl was not the only expensive diversion that I had that summer because Rose decided that getting knobbed by her toyboy was not enough, and she announced that we needed to go out more. What she meant was that *she* wanted *me* to take her out more – the *we* part was just added for effect. So with both Rose and Xochitl pestering me to squire them around my wallet began to take a serious hammering that summer of 1989.

Svetlana

Most people did not have mobile phones back then so I remember the irritation that I felt when someone knocked on my door and said that I had a phone call. Picking up the receiver a man's voice came over the line asking me to confirm my name. Then he mentioned a few mutual acquaintances, people who had given him my name, and then he went on to offer me £50 plus expenses a night cash in hand to drive a whore around London and make sure she did not get up to any mischief!

To say that the idea was jaw-dropping would be to put it mildly. I had never heard of such a thing, and why would anyone want to go to the expense of providing a trollop with a car and driver?

The explanation was that I would be driving a Russian girl around. Now today we are used to Russian whores everywhere, but they were a genuine novelty in 1989. Svetlana was one of the first to make her way illegally to the UK and had quickly started earning a living on her back. Although the Russians had only been in London for a couple of months they had already built up a reputation for chicanery, but they were popular with the customers, all of whom seemed to want their knobs polished by a Russian girl. So the agencies could not just get rid of them, but the classier ones hired men like me to drive them around and generally keep an eye on them.

I must have sounded dubious about the offer because my interviewer came out with the deal-making clincher: I could have a freebie with the girl of my choice once a week. How could I refuse such an offer? So that evening I took my car over to the central London agency to be introduced to Svetlana, my new charge.

Fellows, she was a shagging man's delight! Twenty-two years old, tall and slim, with blonde hair that hung in great waves right down to her bum. Since the colour was natural I remember thinking that to get to that shade of blonde a passing German soldier had to have taken a fancy to Sveta's grannie back in the day.

Taking delivery of Svetlana I could feel my cock perking up at the sight of her as she climbed into my car, displaying rather a nice amount of leg as she did so. I remember thinking that this job was going to be a dream, which is a pity as it turned out because by the end of the day Svetlana and I cordially loathed each other.

The problem was that from the start she was trying to pull a fast one and to make matters worse she tried to involve me in her wheeze, running her fingers over my cock and whispering that if only I would do this or that then all the riches of the earth would be mine. I told her that I wasn't interested and she refused to accept that and redoubled her efforts to seduce me.

"You vant fuck me, don't you? I can tell the vay you look at me," she breathed.

"I will fuck you," I told her by way of reply.

"No, not unless we become partners," she retorted, before leaning over to breath heavily into my ear. Say what you like about the Ruskies, but nobody can accuse them of subtlety.

I let her babble on and the very next day I wandered into the agency and told the old bawd who managed the place that I wanted Svetlana as my freebie. You can imagine Sveta's face when she entered the room to find me, bollock naked and rampant waiting for her.

Obviously, she hated me for that, which was fine because by then I did not like her all that much, either. On the other hand you don't have to like a woman to fuck her so long as she has a nice juicy pussy. Come on, fellows, you know it's the truth.

Gradually Svetlana stopped complaining about my failure to dance to her tune and I stopped teasing her about having to give me for free that which she had offered up as a bribe, and we sort of became friends. She would either occasionally call me up or sometimes even arrive at my student room when she was after something. I would give her a poke and then drive her wherever she wanted to go, or feed her in a nice restaurant.

As the summer of 1989 reached its height my course was about to come to an end and with it the state's largesse, so I needed to decide what I was going to do for money once that terrible day of reckoning arrived. Rosa offered me a job at her college and told me that I could use the little flat, which was nice of her you have to admit. I was mulling the idea over when the gates of hell opened to release several demons all of whom were carrying large buckets of shit which they then proceeded to pour all over me.

Shit Day, as I now call it, began normally enough with me returning from my shower in my bath robe to find Svetlana in my room, smoking one of my cigarettes, having helped herself to a coffee from the percolator that I kept on my writing desk.

"I vish to go to Brighton. How far is Brighton?" Say what you like about Sveta, but she never beats about the bush.

"I dunno, a couple of hours from London by car," I told her.

Svetlana pursed her lips, and then considered her position for a moment. Finally, her mind made up, she reached inside my bath robe and took my cock in her hand. With a few expert pulls she quickly had me standing to attention and then she set to work with a good steady stroking rhythm that made me groan with pleasure.

"You gif me ride to Brighton and I gif you good hand job."

"Fuck that – I give you a ride and you give me a full fuck. A ride for a ride, darling."

"You haf condoms?"

Of course she had her own as a trollop without condoms is like a carpenter without his saw, but it was a worth a try on her part. I was about to push her away and tell her no deal when she came up with a decent compromise.

"I gif you blow job and swallow the come."

"OK, and I give you a ride to Brighton but you pay the petrol."

"Nyet, but I gif you extra blow job in car going to Brighton."

"It's a deal – get sucking."

Thus are matters settled by two people who understood each other perfectly. Sveta got on her knees, gave me back the remains of my cigarette, and then swiftly sucked me down the road to glory. Her tongue flickered over my cock head and then she took the whole shaft in her mouth in one deft deep throat move, before moving on to let her tongue slither along the canal that runs along the underside of a man's weapon. I suppose that most men have been sucked off by their wives and girlfriends, but trust me when I say that unless you have placed your tool in the mouth of a genuine professional then you have really never been sucked at all.

I tried to hold back the tidal wave, but Sveta was too cute for that. She had been fondling my balls throughout and when she felt them begin to move as the hot syrup inside them began to boil, then she redoubled her efforts until the gates opened and the surge began. And I came...

Svetlana climbed to her feet and we arranged our little Brighton trip. Once she had left I quickly got dressed and had breakfast before wandering off to the car park to pick up my vehicle and drive it over to Rose's college. The plan was to teach a class and then give Rose a lesson of a more intimate nature. With that in mind, I fired up the engine, slipped the car into gear, and headed off to the college.

I could tell that Rose was frisky because she kept coming into my class on various spurious pretexts to give me an order or two. Then, during a coffee break she grabbed the three or four teachers who were around and gave us a lecture on some failing or other. Not that I was taking a blind bit of notice as I was too busy admiring the way she strutted backwards and forwards in her trademark high heels, a fitted black red pinstriped skirt clinging to her rounded buttocks. Occasionally she would pause and cross her arms over her puppies to ask if we were all on the same page or working to the same programme?

God know where she got the dialogue from but it was days like that which made me a confirmed believer in feminism. Just the sheer joy of taking orders from a woman all day and then fucking her brains out all night is something that previous generations had never experienced. Today, of course, women like Rose are common but they were still a bit of a novelty in 1989 and believe me the performance never failed to give me a serious hard-on.

So much of a turn on was it that I found it hard to concentrate on the remainder of my class and as soon as it was over I went looking for Rose with a view to riveting her rigid even though the place was full of people. She must have had the same idea because the secretary gave me a note which simply said "flat" so I took my raging stand upstairs to find Rose waiting for me in the bedroom.

"Close the door," she said, her voice thick and heavy. I did just that and then I walked towards her as she stretched out her arms for our embrace.

We kissed each other hungrily, and my hands went down her body to take that firm luscious rump in my grasp. I ran my hands all over it and felt Rose's suspender belt through the material of her skirt. I pulled the garment up around her waist and cupped her pussy in my hand. It was so hot I couldn't believe that she could be ready for me so I slipped my gingers inside her black knickers to check. Yes, oh yes, she was more than ready for my cock.

I stripped Rose of her panties and balled up the frothy confection to hold up to my nose to smell its sweet fragrance, which was a mixture or Rose's perfume and the woman herself.

"Nooo," she said, in mock outrage. "Give them to me!"

I threw the knickers down and pushed Rose onto the bed. Quickly I unhooked my belt, unzipped my trousers then then pushed them down.

Within seconds I was between her thighs and then without any further help my cock just seemed to find its own way into the opening in Rose's thighs and with one push I was home.

She lifted her legs to ease my passage and I began to have her, slowly at first, but then building up the velocity to the killing strokes as Rose urged me on to fuck her harder, harder, and harder.

I lifted myself up on my arms so that I could look down at her and I saw her with her shoes still on her feet and her skirt around her waist and her white blouse still tucked into that skirt. It was a wonderful sight, that of a businesswoman with her clothing in partial disarray as she was given a good fucking. It was that sight more than anything else that drove me close to the edge.

"I can't hold it any longer," I cried.

"Don't, don't hold it! Give it to me! Fill me up!

So I did. I increased the speed and the come juice began to flow for the second time that day.

We lay quietly in each other's arms, but not for as long as was normal after a bout had ended. Rose tried to push me away, but I was too fagged out to even consider moving, so she contented herself with just the words that were aching to be said:

"What have you been up to?" Her question was spoken quietly, but there was an air of menace in it, which made the hairs on the back of my neck stand up.

"What do you mean?"

"You have been with someone else today. You only came a drop and I can smell her on you! I thought that the stench was from one of the students in class, but it isn't is it?"

Rose managed to push me off and she sat up on the bed with a look of cold fury on her face.

"Who is it? That red nigger bitch from Mexico? She's been telling everyone that she sleeps with you!" Rose paused to collect her thoughts and then she hit me with what amounted to the clincher: "You gave her a spanking, didn't you?"

My face must have registered surprise, because Rose clambered out of bed and smoothed down her skirt. She clenched both her hands into fists and jammed them on her hips, and stood there, legs apart, to face me.

"You stupid, northern shit! She is gloating about you all over the fucking college. Telling everyone what you get up to. You took her back to your college room and spanked her, and then you fucked her," she said, pausing only for a moment to take a breath. "She doesn't give a shit about you. This isn't about you, this is about her and me, don't you understand?"

Did I understand? Of course not! What Rose said made no sense to my logical male brain. I shook my head in bewilderment.

"Look," Rose went on, with an air of exasperation. "There are some women who just have to go head to head with other women about men. They see a woman with a man and they have to take him. Then when they have him, they don't want him. It's a power kick for them."

Her words tailed off and then she suddenly started to sob. I waited until the worst was over and then I took her in my arms and spoke to her quietly:

"Rose, you have a husband and family. Have I ever asked you not to be fucked by your husband?"

"Is that because you don't give a damn what I get up to when I am not with you?" Jesus, this was turning into a soap opera, it really was.

"Listen, I will handle the matter, just trust me," I said, trying to reassure her.

"I need the money that the little third world cow brings in. She and all of them. What are you going to do?"

"I am going to have a serious talk with that young madam, you mark my words."

As I drove over to see Xochitl, the idea came to me that since she only had another two weeks in the country before she went back to Mexico I would ask her to kindly keep her mouth shut for that length of time. I would then keep away from the college during working hours and everything would be fine. I could see Rose on our usual days, and Xochitl and Svetlana at other times. All in all it struck me as a rather civilised solution to the problem – more fool me for thinking that anything is ever simple where women are concerned.

I arrived at Xochitl's rather nice service flat and parked the car in her bay. I can distinctly remember pausing to spark up a cigarette before strolling across the carpark to the building's entrance without a care in the world. Xochitl had given me the code that opened the main door and I wandered in to the main hallway and then up the stairs to her first floor flat without any inkling that things were about to go pear-shaped.

"Hello, my love, it is wonderful to see you," said Xochitl as she let me in to her flat. Yes, I remember thinking, we really have to work on that conversational manner to avoid sounding so wooden. Still, she did look rather sweet wearing only her oversized T-shirt that doubled as a nightgown.

"We have a problem," I told her after the great smacking kiss was over.

"What?"

"Rose knows about us. Any idea how that came about?"

"What do you mean by that?"

Whenever a woman answers a question with a question alarm bells should start ringing in a man's head. It means that the little darling has something to hide and she is angling to find out what you know so that she can trim her story accordingly. Alas it does not work with me...

I sat Xochitl on my knee for a spot of gentle interrogation. Yes, it emerged that she had told a few close friends about our affair. A few close friends? Well, actually most of the female students at the college. And the female teachers. And the secretary. Had she heard rumours about my affair with Rose? Of course not and perish the thought! Well, actually she had heard a few rumours and Rose and I had been seen out and about by a secretary's second cousin who just happened to be...

As always with a woman the prattle just seemed to be never ending, but the gist of it was that Xochitl had been blabbing all over town so of course Rose had been given the full story, probably be several people.

There was really nothing more to say, was there? With a sigh I pushed Xochitl off my lap and stood up to leave.

"Where are you going? Women do ask the daftest questions at times, they really do.

"I am off to sort out the mess that you have helped to create with Rose."

"You are leaving me to go to her – you can't do that!" To prove her point Xochitl wrapped her arms around my neck and began to nuzzle my ear.

I tried to get her off me, but the more I untangled her from me the greater became her efforts to remain tangled.

"Listen, you bad bitch, the trouble that you have caused probably can't be fixed, but I am going to have a try."

"Yes, yes, I am a bad bitch and I am a very, very sorry bad bitch." Xochitl looked up at me with her head slightly down, so that she had to turn her eyes right up. The effect was a delight, as it was meant to be.

"Listen, young lady, if I do carry on with you then there must be no repetition of your silliness, do you understand me?

"Yes I do. I am very sorry. Are you very angry with me for being bad?"

"What do you think?"

"What are you going to do to me?"

"What do you think?"

I took Xochitl's arm and marched her over to the sofa. Sitting down I yanked her across my knee, cocked that all-important right thigh over her already scissoring thighs, and quickly clamped her arms behind her back. Then I raised that oversized T-shirt and left the cotton bunched up around her waist. The white thong that she was wearing gave her bottom no protection at all, but be that as it may it had to come down just to teach madam that whoever was in charge it was not her.

She began to wriggle like an eel even before the first smack had landed, but once it had then the wriggling was joined by some pretty frantic kicking. It was all a waste of effort, of course, because I had her firmly in position and she was going nowhere until I decided that the spanking was over.

Although I say it myself, I laid that smacked bottom on with great gusto. First one cheek and then the other came in for the attention of my palm that cracked down with all the force of my arm behind it. I can distinctly remember that going from the top of her rump to the bottom was three smacks on each cheek and spanked Xochitl with groups of six smacks, to cover her whole bottom with my hand and then start the procedure all over again.

I built up a steady spanking rhythm and for the next few minutes the only sound in the room was the crack of my hand against Xochitl's defenceless buttocks and her squeals of anger, outrage and then, finally, her tears of bitter remorse. Normally I bring a spanking to a close when the recalcitrant female who is on the receiving end bursts into tears but that day's spanking was a special event so my arm continued to rise and fall as Xochitl's howls gave way to great gulping sobs and eventually she stopped wriggling and her legs ceased to kick and she lay across my knee, thoroughly chastised and totally humbled.

My arm was aching when I dumped Xochitl onto the floor and lit a cigarette as she howled her cries of tearful remorse into the carpet. I sat there quietly letting my weary arm rest whilst Xochitl went through the usual female performance of sobbing her heart out, obviously in a futile attempt to gain sympathy.

Eventually, about the time I stubbed out the remains of the cigarette, Xochitl's sobs lessened and I was able to pick her up and carry her off to bed.

I will not pretend that it was the greatest sex that I have ever had, because it was the third time around for me that day, but I don't think that I let either myself or England down with my performance. Xochitl certainly moved around rather nicely, although her burning buttocks may have contributed to that movement. When it was all over we lay in each other arms and fell asleep.

It had gone dark when the telephone rang and I simply heard Xochitl pick up the receiver and tell someone that of course she would pass on the message.

"That was Rose," she told me. She said that you should not forget your class tomorrow morning."

I looked into Xochitl's face and saw a butter would not melt in her mouth expression on it and I decided that it was all too much effort. So I turned over and went back to sleep. Tomorrow could take care of itself as far as I was concerned.

Xochitl duly left the country at the end of the month and I did not see her very much during her remaining few days. I tried to suggest a few ideas to her, but she put me off with one lame excuse after another. On the bright side she did not ask me to take her anywhere and I did get a couple of pokes before she left so I cannot really complain too much. At the same time as all that was going on, Svetlana went off to bang her brains out in another part of the city, so that left me free to try and repair the damage done to my affair with Rose. My task was not made any easier by the fact that I had no clear idea why she was so upset. To be honest, given that she was married, what was she complaining about if I had a couple of extra pokes as well? And as for her theory about Xochitl, well, that was just silliness, I reasoned.

The problem was that although Rose and I continued to see each other for another month or so, the joy had clearly gone out of things as far as she was concerned. I remember one night when we were making love she turned her head to one side and looked at the wall, completely oblivious to what was going on.

I became immediately concerned that something had happened to my cock, otherwise why was she not taking her pleasure from it? I asked her about it and she smiled a mirthless smile and told me that it was just the same as normal. Thinking that she had got bored with the position I switched her around for a doggie style fuck, but she said that was not what she wanted. Thinking quickly I remembered that she liked me sat up on the edge of the bed with her sat with her back to me, so she could watch herself being fucked like that in the mirror. I got her into position and everything seemed to be fine until Rose broke down in tears which rather brought the proceedings to a halt.

With a sigh I went and fixed us both a whisky and soda, and lit two cigarettes. Then I waited a moment until Rose had taken some of the drink and followed by a long pull on the cigarette. Then she looked at me tearfully.

"The romance has gone," she said, very quietly.

I shook my head, not understanding. I was still thinking that something had gone wrong with my cock, so why had Mills and Boone suddenly been brought into the equation?

"The romance, the joy, the delight – call it what you want. It was there, with you," she said, gesturing at me. "I have sex with my husband on Friday or Saturday evenings, usually. Never both. He wears blue and white striped pyjamas," she went on irrelevantly. "And takes the trousers off when he wants sex."

"Did you see yourself leaving him for me?"

Rose shook her head.

"Then how can you complain about me fucking someone else?"

"I can't," she had the honesty to reply. "But you have taken the romance out for me."

So that was that. What can you say about bloody women? Rose was opening her legs for her husband and me, but when I did a spot of extra-curricular activity she went all precious on me. That said, we never formally split up and we carried on seeing each other until my Certificate in Further Education was awarded to me, then the whole affair just sort of fizzled out.

As I stood at the end of another decade, my life as a student was about to end as well. I could look back with pride to that New Year's Day a decade earlier when I had vowed that my life would be turned around and I knew that I had certainly achieved that aim. I had known many women during those years, and the most important ones I have just told you about, but I think it fair to say that in all my affairs and flings everyone had clearly understood who wore the trousers in the relationships. I really had put the agonising, humiliating two years of 1980 and 1981 behind me and I could look to the future with confidence.

Looking ahead to that future, I would enter it with a freshly minted set of academic credentials, but no job. So, for reasons that would be as tiresome to explain as they would be to read, but which had nothing to do with Xochitl, I decided that I would go to Mexico, a country where I spent the next two decades. At least the beer was cold and the women were the exact opposite.

CHAPTER SEVEN

Making Videos in Two Countries

Needless to say, my change of country did not lead to any great change in me, and I did everything in Mexico that I had previously done in England, with the only difference being that I did them all in Spanish. Well, most of them in Spanish, as my introduction to the world of video making came about quite by chance, and in a very roundabout sort of way, when I was in London.

The England Experience

I found myself back in the UK during the mid-1990s for several months and an old writer friend mentioned that there was an outfit called Moonglow which made spanking videos and also had a small monthly magazine. The owner was finding that running the magazine was time consuming and he was on the look-out for an editor. Having been in Mexico for almost five years by that time I was out of touch with events in the UK, and I had never heard of either Moonglow or its magazine, so I asked to be put in touch with its owner.

It turned out that there wasn't a magazine as such; rather what existed was a newsletter that circulated to subscribers. It contained information about videos, news of forthcoming parties, as well as a small amount of fiction and the usual readers' letters page. All in all it could have been produced by a local community group had it not been for its theme. Certainly the newsletter could not afford a full-time editor and probably didn't really need a part-time one either. It looked as if this avenue led to a dead end.

That was when the owner began to open up and admitted that finding men for his spanking videos was not the easiest task in the world. The videos needed mature fellows with a degree of gravitas who would not freeze up on camera. Most men who had those attributes also had positions within society and did not need the bad publicity that would ensue if the News of the World found out about their extra-curricular activities. He asked me if I was interested in earning fifty quid plus expenses and when I told him that I was, we arranged to meet the following month at a small film studio in London.

I duly arrived on time to film my part in an epic that I later discovered was called *Rattan College 3*, and to say that I was amazed by what I saw is putting it mildly. Up to that point all my experience in the trade had been as a writer, trying to persuade thuggish individuals with tattoos up their arms to pay me on time. Now I was surrounded by people who looked like they were part of a rather twee Home Counties camera club, and a particularly badly run one at that!

In the first place I was amazed to see that that the shoot was to be without a script. When I queried this with the owner my question was airily brushed aside as being of no importance. Clearly this fellow had been much influenced by the French Cinéma Vérité School, or something. I asked if we were to develop characters as we went along? With the air of a true Christian martyr, the owner told me that I was playing the role of a headmaster and my job was to give a stern lecture to each girl in turn and then get her across my knee for knickers down spankings. And don't bugger about before doing each one, as some of us have homes to go to. So much for cinéma vérité.

My new friend acted as director, cameraman, sound man and brew lad all rolled into one, which was probably a good thing as the studio was so tiny that more people would not have fitted in. It was nothing more than a square room with one corner taken up by a sitting room set and the other a classroom. A third corner was the entrance and through that there was small kitchen just before the main door that led to the street. The fourth was the best as it was filled with about half a dozen chairs, all occupied by men who had paid to watch the shoot.

In theory everything should have gone swimmingly with three of the four girls who I was working with that day arriving at hourly intervals to video their scenes. The fourth was there all the time since she was doubling up as the buffet lady…

"Julie, it's time to be caned."

"Just as soon as I've got these sausage rolls out of the oven."

Needless to say it all turned into chaos, with the girls arriving in their own good time and the shoot dragged on into the evening. The lights made the tiny, overcrowded set even hotter than it would otherwise have been and to cap it all a girl named Karen finished her shoot, went off to get some food in the kitchen, and then came back to announce that she was leaving – thus ruining an otherwise flawless take that was being shot. Needless to say, the young madam was promptly bent over and given six of the very best for her irresponsibility, but it still meant more work for the rest of us.

"That's a wrap!" When we heard those magic words everyone on the set just let out an enormous sigh. The lights were switched off, the camera was packed away, and those of us who were up for it made our way to the nearest pub for a pint or three.

As an introduction to the British way of making spanking videos that day could not have been bettered. I don't know if things have improved since then or if the Great British tradition of muddle through and mend still holds sway, but I have to admit that it was all good fun. I just wasn't sure that I wanted to have to go through the same performance when it came time to shoot my own videos in Mexico, that's all.

My first Mexican video came about almost by accident and it was intended as nothing more than a punishment, or rather as a part of one. And even that only occurred on the spur of the moment.

Mexico and Marina

Marina and I met in late 1997 when I was a 41 year old working at a university in Mexico City and Marina was a student aged 19. Mexico is nothing like England so bedding a female student is no big deal, but alas for me I didn't take into account the pecking order, and I managed to annoy a senior figure who wanted her for himself. With my usual lack of tact I just shouldered my way past everyone with my "excuse me, excuse me, get out of my fucking way, cos this one's mine" air about me and left that very senior figure with his dick in his hand. Oh well, if he reads this then he can rest assured that I stretched Marina's pussy on many occasions over the years that we were together and he need not worry that she was not well seen to. Ahem… Enough of this merry banter: let us continue with our discussion of la cosa nostra.

We arranged to meet the first time in the university's car park. I need to point out at this juncture that le tout Mexico would not be seen dead in public transport so just about every student arrives in their own car and thus the car park was spread over several acres of space. Anyway, we managed to miss each other, at least that was Marina's version of events, but I have always believed that she mixed up the time and actually didn't show up.

The second attempt came a day or so later and involved a rather nice restaurant called Sanborne's which is part of a countrywide chain. At least I could sit down and smoke in air-conditioned comfort, which was a good thing because Marina did not show up that day, either.

I checked my e-mail as soon as I got home – hard though it is to believe, but most people in 1997 did not have a mobile 'phone – and read her litany of excuses that all seemed to involve a silly girl getting lost by taking a succession of wrong turns. So we made a third date and I told her quite simply that if she was even late, never mind failing to show up, I was going to smack her bare bottom hard. Marina swallowed hard and nodded her head as that information was relayed to her, but I don't think that she really believed me, which was a pretty big mistake on her part when you think about it.

The good news is that Marina actually turned up the third time, but the bad news for her bottom was that she arrived about half an hour late. The Mexicans, like most native peoples, have a very free and easy attitude to time, so when madam did show up, wafting expensive perfume in her wake, it was with an air of total nonchalance on her exquisitely carved features.

After the usual air kissing that Mexicans love so much, Marina sat down and fished a Virginia Slim out of her handbag – Gucci, of course. She then sat in front of me with a big grin on her face, waiting for me to light her cigarette for her, which I duly did, concealing my own grin with some difficulty.

"What are we going to do?" Marina was all wide-eyed and enthusiastic and she sent away the waitress with a practised wave of her hand.

"I plan to take you to Tlalpan," I replied, naming one of the main avenues that lead into the centre of Mexico City.

"Tlalpan? What are we going to do there?"

"We are going to a hotel."

"Really?" Marina began to wriggle deliciously in her seat at the thought.

"Yes," I told her, as I signalled for my bill. "Or would you prefer it if I smacked your bare bottom here and now?"

"Nooo! What have I done? You can't be serious!"

Alas for Marina's bottom, I was very serious indeed.

I loaded her into my car and headed off the short distance to Tlalpan and its famous hotels. For those of you who don't know much about Latin types all you really need to know is that they live in enormous family groups where privacy is at a premium. Thus the lovers' hotels which rent rooms *por un rato* – for a short while – usually three hours. Contrary to what you may think most of these places are light, spacious and very clean and the one that I had in mind provided a perfect setting in which to teach a young lady to arrive on time in future.

The car was parked in the underground car park and I decanted Marina from it. Then on impulse, and only because I was worried that it might be stolen, I grabbed my video camera bag that was resting on the back seat and slung it over my shoulder.

"What are you carrying in there?"

"A video camera."

"Oh – that's nice. Are you going to make a video?" She could say the daftest things could that girl. It was on the tip of my tongue to answer her honestly, and say that it was just to avoid having my camera stolen, but the devil got inside me and on the spur of the moment I decided to record the event:

"Yes, I am going to video you having your bare bottom smacked."

"Nooooo!"

"Yes, my dear," I told her as I marched her slowly to the short flight of stairs that led to reception. We had to walk slowly because Marina was trying to dawdle when she wasn't pulling away from me. A firm smack to the rump had her wincing, but put paid to most of her antics and at least I could get her to reception. Once there I paid for the room, collected the key, took Marina by the arm again and walked her to the lift.

Our room was on the third floor and was fairly typical of the Tlalpan hotels – I sometimes get the feeling that they are all built to a standard pattern. A large bathroom led off to the left of the main door as we walked in, then a short passage with a mirror and table taking up one wall, and finally the bedroom itself with about half the space taken up with the giant king sized bed that had a mirror in the ceiling above it. At the foot was an armchair and on the other wall a dressing table and stool. That was about it, as you can forget closets and coat hangers in those places since nobody brings any luggage.

Marina started to giggle with that same deliciousness that she had displayed at the restaurant as she looked at the bed.

"What are you going to do?" she asked, although she already knew the answer.

"I am going to put you over my knee, lift up your skirt, take down your panties, and then smack your bare bottom very hard," I told her, trying my best not to smile.

Marina stuck her lower lip over the upper one. She looked so funny that I could not stop laughing.

"What's so funny?"

"You look like a moose," I told her.

"A moose? How do they look?"

I stuck out my lower lip by way of an answer and Marina dissolved into a fit of giggles. She shook her head and then wrapped her arms around my neck.

"I am going to call you Moose," I said. And I did, too, and still do to this day.

"But don't spank me… At least not very hard," Marina pleaded, doing her best not to show her excitement.

"Listen to me, young lady," I replied, trying my best to be stern. "I decide when you are going to be spanked, I decide how hard it will be, and I decide when it is over – understand?"

I set up the camera and switched it on. As soon as she saw me descending upon her Marina went back into moose mode, with the lower lip firmly planted above its counterpart above. She tried to dig her heels into the carpet so I just grabbed her arm once again and stepped backwards until my legs rested against the bed. Then I sat down, pulling the Moose next to me on the bed where she sat looking delightfully nervous.

I gave her a few moments to allow the reality of the situation to sink in and then I pulled her across my knee, almost immediately locking her thighs in position with my right leg. As I did that I brushed her dark gray woollen skirt up to reveal an exquisitely rounded bottom, tightly encased in black bikini panties. These I peeled down to mid-thigh and was rewarded with a yelp and squeal as the frothy confections were lowered to leave Marina's red-brown bottom totally unprotected.

I gave the bottom a friendly pat – well, I thought it was friendly, but Marina obviously didn't as she yelped a protest and tried to cover her bottom with a hand. Silly girl as it was the work of a moment to take her wrist in my free hand and fold it into the small of her back.

"No, now, we can't have you covering your bottom, can we? How can I spank you if your hand is in the way?" I thought that my questions were quite reasonable, and still do come to think about it, but all Marina did was wriggle like an eel across my lap, all the while giggling and complaining in equal measures. Females – what can you do with them?

Well, what I did with that particular female was spank her, not to soundly, but firmly enough to teach her who wore the trousers in that budding relationship. I remember giving her six vigorous slaps, alternating first one cheek and then the other, and pausing between each smack to let the sensation creep into Marina's flesh as I took control of her across my knee.

"I hurts!"

"Of course it hurts, you silly girl," I told her, ever the teacher to my young pupil.

"Then stop it," Marina yelped, wriggling like a very wet and slippery eel indeed to break free.

"Remember what I told you? I decide when your spanking is over," I said, landing a further half dozen smacks on those luscious bottom cheeks. I wasn't angry with her, not really, but I still don't think it did her any harm to think that her behaviour had earned her a sounder spanking than would otherwise have been the case.

Marina stopped struggling and lay across my knee like a good girl should, so I brought her spanking to a close. She had received about fifty smacks, firmly laid on, but not punitively so and was smiling sweetly when I let her up. Give the girl credit but she gave me a lovely kiss and then put her arms around my neck.

I sent her off to stand in the corner for a while and once I had got her into position facing the wall with her skirt held up to show off her freshly smacked bottom I switched off the camera and then sat back and lit a cigarette to enjoy the show. Marina stood very quietly, with only the occasional glance behind her to make sure that neither my hand nor I were anywhere near her glowing behind.

With a final lingering look at the bottom that I had just corrected I went and picked up the camera to rewind the tape inside. Sitting in a chair I was quite happily watching the action replay when I heard a little voice from over on the bed:

"Are you going to keep me waiting long?"

I looked around and saw that madam had stripped herself naked and climbed into bed. And there was me thinking that she was a sweet little girl who would need to be coaxed into bed, instead what I had was a minx who clearly understood how to weigh up a man's balls with just one glance. I must have said as much to Marina who promptly began to count off the number of cocks that she had ridden thus far – at least it gave me time to get undressed and clamber into bed. The problem was that she still didn't shut up about her previous rides once I was naked and next to her...

"And then there was Pedro, he's at la Universidad del Valle now, and he is very, very Catholic and gets horribly upset at what we do together. He wants to be a priest and I think he worries that I may send him to hell or something..."

On and on she rattled and the only way to shut such a woman up is to fuck her so I did. I pushed Marina onto her back, climbed aboard her and placed my cock in her hand.

"Oh, you're ready," she squealed, gripping my hardness firmly. "So am I," she announced, placing my cock into the entrance to paradise.

We made love, and it was quite simply wonderful. There was no hurry and we talked as we fucked, with Marina breaking off from time to time to nibble my neck, something which I find irresistible, and which many other woman have had to be told to do, but which Marina did instinctively – I told you that she was made for the bedroom, didn't I?

We were together for some years and still keep in touch from time to time. I helped her find work as an English teacher and she quickly began to supplement that with activities of a more intimate nature involving the wealthy executives that she taught. Today she divides her time between Mexico City and Miami, where she spends about a week every month, as the very personal assistant to an American businessman.

Let's wish her luck, shall we?

You are wondering how the clip ended up all over the web, aren't you? I set up a Yahoo spanking group in Mexico, the clip was uploaded to that site, and from there other Spanish language groups picked it up. Eventually I made other clips and put them all onto a disk, which was offered for sale in Mexico, and bit by bit the videos leaked out into the web where people began to pass them around as freebies. The quality of the videos that I made in Mexico is not up to today's standards. Still, the Marina video is not a bad little clip and she did look very sweet across my knee with her bottom on display. Being a Mexican her bottom is naturally as red as the rest of her, but I am pleased to say that I reddened it a bit more that day!

Victoria

There was no market for clips in those days to speak of as everybody bought full length videos. I didn't fancy the idea of shooting a 50 minute epic, as I doubted if I would be able to have found the cameraman, as well as the lighting and sound fellows who would be needed for such a shoot. To make matters worse I did not even have the equipment so a camera and lighting rig at least would have to have been hired, with all that cost then being lost if the Mexican girls decided to stay at home that day. This is a scenario not unheard of in England and one very common in Mexico where indolence is a national pastime.

I thought that maybe a one hour compilation disk would sell so I set out to find the two or three girls who would be needed to make it. Since I would just be working with one girl at a time the technical problems would be less as I could operate the camera myself for a short clip. Anyway, full of enthusiasm for the new project I set out to get the ball rolling and that was when the dead hand of Mexican inertia kicked in and nothing got started.

The main problem that I had was with the putative actresses. I first got in touch with girls in the Mexican scene and quickly realised that the reason why they are in the scene, as opposed to bringing up a platoon of children like 99 percent of Mexican women do, is that they were wealthy. The internet is a rich person's toy in Mexico and a few dollars here and there was no big deal to the type of girl who went to Paris to buy her handbags, for instance.

So I hit the agencies where the American porn companies find their models, these being the girls that you see in the anonymous stock footage. A lot of that is shot in Mexico because the girls are cheaper to hire than they are in the USA, so I figured that if they will spend a day getting fucked for around fifty quid then they would jump at the chance of a spanking for a ton, right?

Wrong! Every girl I spoke to explained that it was one thing getting her pussy stretched or her bum hole widened for $100 or so a day, but a spanking sounded like hard work to them, and the fee that they angled for was ludicrously high. Besides, as one girl pointed out, she could always hit the bars after work and pick up a tourist if she was short of cash that week, so why bust a gut with me?

It was looking as if my career as a Mexican pornographer was going to end before it had begun, which was when in desperation I hit the seedy bars where the ficheras are to be found. Most Mexican cantinas have these girls and their job is to get the men to buy drinks. Every time someone buys the girl a glass she gets a token, a ficha, which she exchanges for cash at the end of the night. These ficheras will hold your hand, and if you pay them extra they will hold any other part of your anatomy that you fancy, and it really was just a matter of finding one who would agree to go across my knee, I figured.

To be honest it was as easy as falling off a log, and I kicked myself for not thinking of that earlier. The first bar I went into I met Victoria and when I explained the deal to her she agreed with alacrity. I think that I paid her £50 for the shoot and I agreed that she would get lunch afterwards at my expense. At first she was dubious because she thought that I planned to give her a kicking or punch her face, but when I explained the deal totally to her she burst out laughing.

"So, you'll just hit my bottom with your hand?"

"Yes, that's all there is too it. I'll meet you and we'll drive to a hotel. The shoot will take an hour and then we can have lunch. From leaving here to getting back, allow three hours all told," I explained.

Victoria was seriously impressed with this and wanted to do the shoot that day, but I told her that her *ropa de puta* was not acceptable, so tomorrow could she please wear something that a secretary might use to go to work in?

Looking at that first video that I made with here it is obvious that she did me proud the following day. I used a tripod and shot the whole spanking from one angle. Then I let Victoria up and changed the camera angle so that the lens was pointing at her face. Back across my knee she went and the facial expressions were then grabbed as my hand cracked across her bottom. The only problem was that there was no air-conditioning in the hotel that I used and it became damned hot under the video lights and I began to wilt as you can tell if you watch the video closely.

Once the video had been shot then I took some still photographs and once that was done I started to pack all my gear away and when I finished I turned around to find that Victoria had stripped herself naked and climbed into bed. What can I say? She just automatically expected that for that kind of money I would expect to fuck her as well. I was tempted to tell her to forget it, but I am an Englishman after all and one doesn't want the natives thinking that we are unable to rise to the occasion, so I scrambled into bed with her and slipped her a damned fine length.

Rather a good day's work when you come to think about it and all for less than a hundred quid all told!

As Victoria and I were leaving the hotel following the making of our little epic I casually mentioned that I planned to shoot another video clip that month and did she know of anyone who might be interested in starring in it? Quick as a flash and in spite of her sorely tried bottom, the good lady announced that actually she quite fancied making another video and when were we going to do it? I gave her my business mobile number and told her to keep in touch, little realising that she would call me every day until I finally agreed to do this second shoot with her.

About two weeks later as we drove to the hotel where the video was to be made I asked the girl if she had enjoyed the previous shoot and she said that she had. Digging a little deeper it emerged that what she really enjoyed was getting what was to her very easy money indeed. She had been with me on the previous shoot for a little over two hours and had walked away with fifty quid in her purse and a decent lunch in her tummy. The fact that she also had a sore backside and a well stretched pussy was neither here nor there: Victoria had calculated that the amount of time and effort she had expended was more than compensated for by the money that she had earned. As she proudly told me, she earned more for her time with me than she would expect to make in a week hustling in the bar.

I have to be honest and say that I really felt that I was doing my bit for Anglo-Mexican relations that day. Not that my warm feeling stopped me from leathering her backside to a fiery shade of red, but I approached my labours that day with a feeling of intense satisfaction as I laid the leather across Victoria's bare bottom.

When it was all over Victoria and I went her to bed as we had the time before, but this time she was quite happy to spend a lazy afternoon with me after the horizontal jog was over. I remember that I ordered food sent to the room and we sat on the bed, with Victoria wrapped in a sheet, and the pair of us munched tacos. All in all rather a nice way to spend an afternoon, the video had been shot without any trouble, my balls had been emptied, then my belly filled, and finally I was lounging around chatting to the model. Is it possible to have a better day?

It gave me a chance to ask the girl about her views on discipline. Normally I don't bother as I just assume that the girls are in it for the money, as indeed am I, but as part of that lazy Mexican afternoon I got Victoria to chat about her previous punishments.

As I had already guessed what had happened in her family was that the father had come home three sheets to the wind after having spent his wages in the cantina and then kicked the living daylights out of the mother if she had asked such obvious questions as what were the tribe going to eat that coming week? Victoria told me rather proudly I thought that her mother had got in the habit of waiting outside the father's workplace until he emerged and then grabbing as much cash of him as she could. It was all a fairly typical tale of life in those United Mexican States in other words. Victoria had married and the saga had continued until her old man took his hook one day and had never returned. She went off to work in a bar to feed herself and her children.

This is why she was so amazed at my offers to her. Compared to long hours hustling drunks for a few pesos a night, with a leavening of a measly few pesos more that came by bedding one of them, the work that she did with me must have left her feeling that she had won a prize that month.

Paloma

During the years that I lived in Mexico I ran a Yahoo group dedicated to our little predilection, indeed it was the first such group set up in Mexico, running in Spanish. Quite a few women got in touch with me via the group seeking discipline and I would always make it clear to them that a red rump was going to be followed by a well worked pussy. Some dropped out, whereas others were only too happy to agree to my terms. A group larger than either of the other two consisted of the women who put forward objections to receiving my cock, but who really only wanted to be held down for the knobbing. Needless to say I was only too pleased to oblige those fine ladies.

Paloma was one of the few females who managed to complete part one of the process without ever proceeding to part two and how she did it was a masterly example of feminine guile in action. She contacted me to discuss a spanking and once she had satisfied herself that I knew what I was talking about and was not all tongue and trousers she set her trap.

She explained that she was interested in video work and went on to enquire, sweetly, if it involved sex. I replied that it didn't necessarily, and went on to explain that an audition would be needed. I should have been wary when she agreed to that with alacrity, and double wary when she suggested a discrete hotel and promised to be in a room waiting for me. Experience should have taught me that when something is too good to be true it invariably is, but greed got the better of me and I wandered off to the hotel on the day in question to find Paloma, a well preserved and incredibly rich looking 30 year old, waiting for me.

She explained that her husband was not a disciplinarian and that should have given me pause for thought because how could such an obviously wealthy married women appear in one of my videos? She also asked me if I wouldn't mind acting as if I were her father and give her a lecture over something or other. That struck me as strange since the aim of the session was just to test out her capacity to receive a spanking, but Paloma explained that she really needed to get into the swing of things otherwise she would not be able to kick her legs like a real naughty girl would. I agreed, obviously I did, because I am truly the whitest of men.

I pushed Paloma into a corner and held her wrists firmly by her side. Speaking softly into her ear I told her in Spanish that she was a bad girl and all the protests in the world would not save her from the retribution to come. At first she struggled, but gradually the fight left her and she stood quietly, head down, awaiting her fate. I was seriously impressed with what I still imagined was her acting talent...

Taking the wretched girl by the arm I marched her over to the bed, sat down and pulled her across my knee. It was the work of a moment to flip up her cotton skirt and peel down her white panties to mid-thigh. Cocking my right leg over her thighs to prevent any bucking and weaving, I proceeded to administer correction to the traditionally seat of learning.

Paloma behaved as any normal girl would under those circumstances. First she wriggled her hips from side to side and then she put her right hand behind herself to try to cover her rapidly reddening buttocks. I grabbed her wrist and folded the arm neatly into the small of her back before continuing the spanking to its conclusion in a crescendo of rapid fire smacks that left Paloma breathless and unable to squeal any more. She lay helpless across my knee, sobbing quietly and utterly unable to resist.

The temptation to proceed to the next stage which involves the thoroughly submissive and obedient little girl receiving a good knobbing was almost too much to resist, and certainly my cock was straining against my trousers in its eagerness to be inside Paloma's no doubt ripe pussy. However, and you may find this hard to believe, but sheer greed got the better of me. I really thought that this bright eyed and bushy tailed young madam was going to be the next star of the spanking video world and I wanted my fair share of the financial action so I left her unfucked to compose herself.

I smoked a cigarette while Paloma blubbered and then went off to the bathroom to do whatever women do at times like that. When she returned a few minutes later she looked none the worse for wear and had a perky smile on her elfin face. That was when I noticed that the lace curtain in the window was blowing gently in the breeze…

I strode across and pulled back the curtain. Looking down from the first floor room I was staring into the courtyard below where the cars were parked and standing around, all smoking and with big grins on their faces were the men of the hotel, the car jockeys, bellboys and the like. I turned to Paloma and gestured for her to come and have a look.

As soon as she appeared in the window a cheer went up from the men below, a cheer that sort of froze in their throats as Paloma gazed steadily from one to the next, quite simply freezing their little balls in their sacks, by gazing at each man in turn, holding his eyes for a moment until he looked away and then going on to the next in line. It was a masterly demonstration of how an upper class Mexican woman keeps the lower orders in their place. Paloma demonstrated a total, patrician contempt for the men, something that they sensed and felt helpless to do anything about. A few minutes later and we were downstairs waiting for two of those same men to bring our cars. During that time Paloma stood quietly, a hand resting on my shoulder, completely oblivious to the people around all of whom knew that her backside was the colour of a tomato and that she would be sleeping on her stomach that night. The cars arrived; Paloma kissed me on the lips and climbed into hers. I was pleased to see her sit down gingerly and she had the good grace to pout at me before she drove off.

I never saw her again. All the contact details that I had suddenly went dead and that was the end of Paloma. Obviously she had played me like a violin to get what she wanted out of me. She used my own greed and desire to make money out of her as a way of blinding me to the game that she was playing until it was too late. That said I don't hold any malice towards her – Paloma was a consummate player and she earned my respect for that. Not only that, but she brought home to a gang of Pedros, Pacos and Panchos just what it means to be a brown-skinned, short-dicked, sad-arsed loser!

That is something that I still chuckle over.

Labouring like this in the hot tropical sun was tough on my Anglo-Saxon body so I quickly adopted the local style of clothing. I became a fan of the short-sleeved version of the guayabera shirt, and my long hair was cropped to a minimalist length. With a broad-brimmed Panama hat on my head I managed to find time to enjoy myself with some of the nation's finer fillies, and not just in Mexico, either. Your humble correspondent spread both himself and his seed around the region, as you will discover in the next chapter.

CHAPTER EIGHT

The Mexico Years, 1990-2010

I called her Blue...

Paloma whom we saw in the last chapter was not the only woman that I met in Mexico who only craved a spanking and decided that I was the cove to administer it; the woman that I used to call Blue was another. I teased her by calling her that as I told her that no man would ever need the blue-coloured Viagra pills when she was around. Just a couple of years younger than me, normally I would not have bothered with a woman that age, but Blue had worn well and was still willowy and lithe in spite of her fifty years. Like Paloma before her she was a creole, a person of European blood, born on that native Mexican shore but not indigenous to it. Unlike her red-brown sisters, with their wide hips and heavy breasts, who are old and worn out from work and childbearing by the time they are Blue's age, this woman had clear, milky skin and a bottom that was pert and firm to the smack.

How we got in touch was reminiscent of Paloma as well as it was via my Yahoo spanking group. Blue made it plain from the start that all she wanted was a spanking and for some reason I went along with her nonsense for about a week. During that time we met twice and her bottom was blistered twice, but as you might expect I felt distinctly unhappy as I hauled my hard-on away at the end of those sessions.

By the time of our third assignation my sanity had returned and as we parked our cars in the hotel's car park I blithely informed madam that on this occasion her buttocks were to burn and her pussy was then to be poked. She started to bluster and came up with all sorts of excuses, but I just turned on my heel and strode off to the reception desk. Glancing back over my shoulder I just told her to march smartly after me and then without further ado I strode purposefully towards the door that led out of the car park and into the reception area, fingers crossed that she would follow. As I opened the door she caught up with me and I just pushed her through and left her to cool her heels whilst I paid for the room.

As we rode up in the lift Blue was almost crying with fury. She sort of spat at me that I could do as I pleased, she didn't care, and all she planned to do was close her eyes and wait for it to be over. I didn't bother replying as I wanted to save my energies for the bout that was shortly to begin.

Getting her into the room did not shut Blue up in the least, which meant that I was in no real mood for pleasantries. She was wearing a blue and white polo shirt with wide white trousers and I simply unbuttoned them, pulled down her zip, spun madam around and yanked both trousers and knickers to her knees. The lady was then pulled across my knee as I sat down on the bed and my right leg was cocked over her thighs to stop any nonsense.

I think it fair to say that this was a memorable spanking. It was not that I was particularly annoyed at Blue, but I was irritated by her attitude. As I soundly spanked first one cheek and then the other, I reflected that the whole point of a spanking is not to hurt the girl's bottom and leave it at that. It is to modify the female behaviour pattern, so that obedience comes from within her. The trick is to close down her options, so that the act of submission becomes the only possible outcome. If a man can get a woman to accept that within her own mind then he is well on the way to success with her.

Blue ceased to struggle, although she managed to prevent herself from crying, and I ended the discipline. I let her fall to the floor, gave her a moment to compose herself, and then I took my semi-hard cock from my trousers, and grabbed a handful of her long blonde hair. Then I put my cock into her mouth and held her head as she sucked it to full hardness.

I picked her up and she looked me in the eyes with a look of utter resignation on her face. I lowered her onto the bed, checked with my finger to see that she was slick and wet, and then I mounted her to begin the slow, remorseless fuck pokes that drove my cock deep into her helpless body. Blue wrapped her arms around my neck, and slowly but surely I built up the rhythm to a killing velocity that had her throwing her head back and making low animal like noises in her throat. A minute or two before I emptied myself into her I felt her bring her thighs together, try to close them, but being prevented from doing so by my own thighs that held hers apart by force. She was coming – when she reached her moment of truth that was what she always did.

Later she told me that she had just had her first ever climax with a man. Her husband was an in-out type of fellow who shot his load very quickly, it seemed. That information gave me a great deal of pleasure then, just as thinking about it gives me an almost equal amount of pleasure now.

Blue was my mistress for almost a year, but she could never get over her guilt at being my lover. To be honest that made her a very unusual Mexican as my experience of the country had taught me that the average person will pretty much follow their instincts, but Blue had those curious western, bourgeoisie values which people like me find fairly risible, but had them she did, and that is why she stopped seeing me.

A paid interlude

There is a danger here that you might think after reading my accounts of Marina, Paloma and Blue that I only ever mixed with the wealthier end of the Mexican female spectrum. Trust me when I say that nothing could be further from the truth. I am, in the fullest of senses, a non-discriminatory swordsman.

You do not believe me, I can tell, so let me tell you a story that will illustrate the point. I remember finding myself on a street called San Pablo in sunny Mexico City when I realised that I was nursing a rather insistent blue-veiner. Luckily, I was on the right street as it is wall-to-wall trollop, so my strides took on another purpose as I looked for a working girl that would put a nice shine to the increasingly hard knob that I carried inside my trousers. I picked out a likely looking lass who was about 20 and wearing a rather fetching black Lycra mini-dress and agreed a price with her. For some reason and no matter what the exchange rate is, a San Pablo harlot including hotel always seems to cost a tenner. Along with haircuts, a leg over is seriously good value in that city.

Off we went to the hotel and once we were there whatever her name was got to work stroking my balls and sucking my cock. I was on my back with the girl at my side and my trousers were down to my thighs when all of a sudden I felt a hand very gently move something around on my left side. Sitting up I saw that the girl had somehow managed to unzip my trousers' security pocket and had partially removed the wallet. Whilst I looked at her she was busily engaged in trying to remove a note with one hand.

I couldn't help but laugh, and the girl's head snapped up as she realised that she had been caught out.

"What are you laughing at?" she said, a look of wide-eyed innocence on her face. Say what you like about Mexican trollops, but they don't confess their sins easily.

"Fancy a trip to the police?" I stood up as I asked her the question and fastened my trousers around my waist, making quite sure that the wallet was back in its zipped pocket. I dragged the girl to her feet, stood her in front of me and repeated the question just to make sure that she got the message.

All she did was shrug. The insolent little shrug, that was followed by a roll of the eyes and a flick of the hair, that Mexican girls of whatever background are experts at giving. A big mistake with me at the best of times and that day was definitely not the best of times to try on the indifference trick.

"Listen, bitch," I said quietly, in a cold monotone so that she could hear every word as I spoke it. "I am a white, foreign, male and I assure you that the cops will listen to me, especially if they think that it might be worth their while. I held up my hand and rubbed my thumb and forefinger together in the international gesture for the act of money changing hands

The girl licked her lips nervously, so I pressed home my advantage. She was from one of the Gulf of Mexico states, that much I could tell from her accent. Veracruz seemed a likely bet so I ran with that one: "Think we should let the people back home in Veracruz know where to find you?"

The girl stepped back and lowered her head. She held her hands in front of her and I could just see through the strands of long black hair that ran down to roughly the level of her bra strap that her mouth was moving as she tried to form words.

"I will do whatever you want and you don't have to pay me," she said in a voice that spoke of defeat and resignation.

"No," I told her. "I will pay you every centavo that I promised you and if you are as enthusiastic in bed as you were grabbing my wallet I might even give you a tip."

The girl looked at me quizzically, her head cocked to one side, hardly daring to hope that everything might end as simply as that. Before she got too cocky I hastened to give her the bad news:

"Now then, about your thieving. For that you get this," and I held out my hand, with the palm up, and then waved it from side to side.

The girl understood immediately so I just sat down and indicated with my right index finger that she should come forward and then I simply pointed to my thigh. Without a word she lay across my lap and it was the matter of a moment to pull up her dress to reveal her very firm buttocks clad in a lilac thong. I then gave her twelve firm smacks on alternate cheeks.

Standing her up again in front of me I saw a look of fury on her face, mixed in with pure, insolent defiance. I could not believe that the bloody woman could be so foolish. I had not actually been all that angry with her and all I wanted to do was have my erection attended to, with the spanking just to remind her not to be so bloody silly in future, and there she was, looking a gift horse in the mouth and just asking for a serious tanning.

Which is what I proceeded to give her. There was no way that I was going to leave her in that mood, and if a fine spanking was what it took to bring her to heel, then a fine spanking was on its way. I pulled the silly little girl back into position across my knee, lifted the dress again and this time I peeled her thong down to mid-thigh. She started to protest and tried to hold onto the garment, but a firm smack to the rump made her let go and the necessary preliminaries were soon completed. I really do not know why women who wear a thong that leaves the bottom bare and gives them no protection at all from a hard male hand still object to the lowering of that garment, but they do. It probably has to do with a desire to keep some measure of dignity, but I am sorry to have to tell you, ladies, that dignity is not allowed with me when discipline has been awarded.

I spanked her soundly, first one cheek and then the other. My right leg was cocked over her kicking thighs and I took her right hand in my left and held it away from her bottom. She tried to use her free arm to lever herself up, but it was a simple matter to jam my left elbow into her back just below the shoulders and keep her down until I decided that the correction had been administered.

This time when I stood her up she was completely chastened and kept her eyes down as I looked into her face. I told her that she was naughty and that her spanking had been made ten times worse by her insolence following the first dozen smacks. I went on to tell her that if anyone else ever had cause to discipline her then she should not be quite so foolish. I also told her to improve her pickpocketing techniques...

The girl nodded her head, saying "Yes sir" in Spanish, over and over again in a quiet voice. I lifted her head and saw the tears forming in the corners of her eyes. With a sigh I realised that she had deployed the weapon that few men can resist so I accepted the reality of that situation and put my arms around her until the sniffles ended. She was a tough Mexican slapper so that did not take long, but for a few brief moments she was a silly little girl who needed a hug, which is what she got.

Once the little local difficulty was over I have to give that girl credit and say that she gave me a very fine blowjob indeed, running her tongue around the head of my cock before deep throating me, all the while holding my balls in her hands and moving them gently through her fingers. Trust me when I say that is did not take me long to shoot and then give her extra credit because she took every drop.

She went off to the bathroom and when I poked my head around the door I saw that she was slowly rubbing her bottom and looking at my handiwork in the mirror. I couldn't help but laugh and to her credit she had spirit enough to pout at me and stick her tongue out.

In case anyone is wondering, I not only paid her, but I left her with a nice tip as well. She had earned her money that day.

Lupita and Molly:
a mother and daughter combination.

I suppose that even for a libertine like me having a mother and daughter combination that involved me spanking the mother, the daughter snorting coke, and then fucking the pair of them takes some doing, and many people over the years have told me that this little history is a fantasy. Actually it really happened, but as with many of the crazier things that have taken place in my life, it could only have happened in Mexico.

In December 1994 the Mexican peso fell through the floor, to be quickly followed by what looked like the whole economy. Credit dried up overnight, debts were called in, and foreclosure became the order of the day as everyone scrambled to salvage what they could from the wreckage. For someone like me who had never trusted the peso and had a stash of dollars handy it was a fun time to be around – certainly my penis was a happy and very busy fellow. You might say that I was rocking around the cock as it were...

One man who was most certainly not rocking was Pedro Perez, as I shall call him. Pedro was tall for a Mexican at about 5' 9" but other than that he was fairly typical dark-skinned wheeler and dealer who looked like he had a lavatory brush glued to his top lip. He had made his way up from the provincial chancer that he still was at heart thanks to various dodgy government deals and now his company looked set to follow everything else down the toilet. Pedro was resigned to a life back in small town Mexico, living on a diet of beans and tortillas which is what he had grown up with.

How our paths crossed is fairly straightforward. Pedro had heard of me as the Englishman who sold spanking videos to wealthy Mexicans or to equally loaded British expatriates, many of whom were involved in the financial sector. Pedro needed a loan to save his swarthy neck and all doors were closed, so desperation drove him to set up a meeting with me. His idea was that I would call my friends and tell them how upright and honourable Pedro was and one of them would then lend him some money. I did tell you he was desperate, didn't I?

Pedro arrived at our lunch meeting in a nice, but not over expensive bar, with a rather blousy woman of about forty at his heel. She was the usual reddish-brown, black-haired, wide hipped female such as Mexico churns out by the million. Needless to say I assumed that he had picked up a tart and looked around for the other one, since bringing one trollop to ease the flow of discussions made no sense at all. Seeing nobody else I opened my mouth to ask where the other whore was just as Pedro took me by the hand, assured me of his gratitude at my agreeing to meet him at such short notice, and could he introduce his wife, Maria Guadalupe, or Lupita to her chums?

So we sat down and I listened to Pedro's ideas. My role in Pedro's grand scheme was obviously going to be pretty minimal since all he wanted me to do was call people and introduce him. Once he had got his foot in the door my job was done. To be honest as the afternoon wore on I felt my weariness grow, Pedro was in no position to offer me very much since he was on his beam end financially. Put another way, what was I getting out of this other than a free lunch and plenty of booze, which by that time I had already had?

Pedro had come prepared for this and with a smile he began to expand on a new theme, that of Lupita and her charms. As he sat back and elaborated on how great she was I realised that my fee was to be an afternoon in bed with the woman. I threw back my head and roared with laughter at the cheek of the man and then I looked at Lupita and saw the look of utter fury in her face and I slapped my thighs in glee.

Pedro got up to go to the lavatory, giving me a conspiratorial wink as he did so. I looked again at Lupita and considered her for a moment. There is really only one thing worse than an old slapper gone to fat and that is a fat old slapper who has had a dose of respectability and can feel it slipping away from her. In spite of her nice clothes and expensive perfume it was obvious that whilst you can take the bar girl out of the bar you can never really take the bar out of the girl. Lupita was basically some grubby little social climber who had hooked her claws into Pedro years before and was now furious at having to go back to her old trade.

I have never forced any woman to do anything that she really does not want to do, but I do enjoy situations like this where a trollop has to spread her thighs because all the other options facing her are even worse than polishing a knob. Grinning all over my face at her discomfort I leaned over and whispered in her ear that we would make the sweetest music together and was rewarded by flashing eyes and a face black with anger at her situation.

"Alternatively," I told her in Spanish, "I could just take my belt to you."

Lupita did not reply but I could tell from the look on her face that our time together was going to be long and memorable.

Two days later found me sitting in a rather nice hotel room waiting for madam to arrive. I had deliberately chosen not to bed her after our earlier meeting as it amused me to give her a couple of days to stew on her predicament. Besides, Pedro had paid for the hotel, so I knew that she would arrive eventually because her loving husband would drag her there if that proved necessary. Sure enough, and only about fifteen minutes or so after the appointed hour – this is Mexico when all is said and done – I heard a firm knock on the door and pausing only to stub out my cigarette I went to answer the summons.

To say that I did a double take as I opened the door is putting it mildly. Instead of seeing fat, forty-something Lupita I was greeted by a svelte vision of loveliness in her very late teens or early 20s. The vision was clad in white moccasins, a seriously expensive pair of jeans that hugged her ripe young frame in all the right places, topped by a white silk blouse that hung outside the jeans and barely contained her delightfully jiggling, melon-like boobs.

"Hola," said the vision. "Soy Fernanda – ¿hablas español?

Without waiting for a reply, she pushed Lupita into the room, walked in immediately behind her and closed the door. To be honest I hadn't even noticed the older woman, oozing out of her dress.

"I speak a little English," she went on switching into that language, with a rather sweet Irish lilt to her accent. "I am the daughter of Pedro and Lupita," she concluded, taking the weight of her body on her right foot and rocking the other one from right to left and back again on the heel.

Looking at both women it was obvious that she was telling the truth. However the difference between them was more than the 20 year age gap. Fernanda had style, and that was something that her mother would never possess. To put Lupita in an English context, it was rather like taking a typical slapper from Middlesbrough, say, dressing her well, and then expecting her to be anything other than a Middlesbrough slapper. Lupita looked as if she should be making the bed, not getting ready to get in it.

Not that she was, by the way. She stood there in what should have been a rather nice silky black dress that was set off with a riot of red rose bud patterns all over it and glowered at me.

Fernanda sighed heavily. "My dad didn't think that mum would go through with it, so I am here to make sure that she does, Fernanda explained with a grin on her face and speaking Spanish obviously for her mother's benefit. Clearly there was no love lost between these two, I decided.

To buy myself some time while I figured the situation out I asked Fernanda where the Irish lilt had come from.

"In Dublin's fair city, where the girls are so pretty," she sang in a rather good voice. "I go there every year for English summer schools," she explained.

"I first set me eyes on sweet Molly Malone," I sang, concluding the song's verse. "I am going to call you Moll from now on," I announced, and so I do to this day, whenever we meet.

The newly renamed girl chortled with delight and went over to the wall to remove a face mirror from its hook which she then placed on a table. She sat down, opened her bag and took out a small envelope. The white powder within it was then put on the mirror and turned into a line with a few deft movements of a banknote. The note was then rolled up and the coke snorted.

Eyes sparkling, Molly looked at both of us, first one and then the other, her grin running from ear to ear. She didn't need to say anything as we both knew that the fucking was about to begin.

So, alas, did Lupita, the star of the matinee performance. She exploded in anger and let rip with a choice tirade of obscene Spanish aimed at her daughter who, it seemed, was letting the side down with her behaviour, which was only fitting in a whore.

With a heavy sigh, as if she carried all the weight of the world on her shoulders, Molly got to her feet, packed away her paraphernalia, and came over to kiss her mother. I thought that was a gesture that fell into the pushing your luck category, but Molly seemed to know what she was doing.

"You are not staying?" My question was genuinely regretful as I had started to wonder if Pedro would swap his wife for his daughter as part of the afternoon delight, but Molly was too fly for that.

"Enjoy yourselves," she said, as she sashayed out of the room, closing the door firmly behind her.

Lupita looked as if she was about to lose the plot completely so angry had she become. I must say that the sight of her like that awakened my interest in her, and since I have always found an angry woman an incredible turn-on, I decided to see what happened when she was thoroughly provoked.

"Speaking about whores, how many cocks did you suck, back when you worked in that fly-blown bar in that shithole of a town back in the north?" My question was not purely speculative as Lupita had a northern accent, and the only way a slapper like that could get on was on her back, and a cantina would be the logical place for the teenage Lupita to meet trade.

My question had the desired effect because madam raised both hands that had been clenched into fists, her head went back, and her mouth opened in a snarl. Clearly she planned to give me some of the same choice language that her daughter had just been treated to.

I didn't give her a chance. I grabbed both wrists, forced them down by her side, and then pushed her back against the wall. The funny thing was that I wasn't even angry. My plan was to calm her down before rutting her, but Lupita by then had become so angry that she wasn't thinking straight. She turned her head to the side so as not to look at me and then she looked down to blank me out of her vision completely.

"Now, now," I told her. "Remember that you are only back in your old trade for an afternoon. Look, even if you don't like me, you can close your eyes and pretend that I am Michael Douglas," I went on, hopefully. "You might even like my cock. It is nice and juicy," I concluded, trying to give her something to look forward to.

You can't talk to some people and I could see that my sweet words were getting me nowhere. I let go of one of her wrists and took her chin in my hand to lift up her face to mine. I felt her muscles clench as she resisted the pressure, then when I proved too strong for her, she tried to turn her head to the side to avoid me that way.

I forced her to look into my eyes and was just about to continue with my sweet reasonableness when Lupita used her free hand to punch me on the side of my head.

To say that was a no-no is putting it mildly. I spun her around, grabbed her by the back of the neck and decided in an instant that this madam was going to be taught a lesson to the traditional seat of learning.

Looking to my left and behind me I saw a rather nice, high-backed chair with two arms that curved down to join the front legs but which had about 18 inches of space between them and the chair's cushion. I decided that the chair would do nicely, and holding Lupita with one hand I began to release my belt from its trouser loops with the other. Then I held it up in front of Lupita's face so that she would know exactly what was about to happen to her, and her eyes widened as the realisation of her predicament dawned on her.

"Now you listen to me very, very carefully," I told her, annunciating every word and speaking in a soft but determined tone. "I am going to put this belt across your arse and you are going to learn your place. It's either that, or I phone Pedro and tell him that you are not performing like a good little whore should. If I do that," I went on remorselessly, "then a sore backside is going to be the least of your worries, isn't it?"

Lupita sagged against me. She didn't say anything and kept her head down, obviously so I couldn't read her face, but I was willing to bet that it had a look of utter resignation on it. I knew that I didn't need to hold her arms anymore and as I let them go she folded them across her ample breasts.

Throwing the belt over my shoulder I simply took Lupita by the arm and marched her to the chair that I planned to bend her over. To say that she skipped merrily to her punishment would be a lie, but she didn't put up the struggle that I expected a wild cat like that to do. She resisted by forcing me to half drag her along, but she walked and did not need to be carried. Her teeth were clenched and she kept glancing at the ceiling as if appealing to whatever god she worshipped to rescue her from what was to follow.

As we got to within a pace of the chair I pushed Lupita forwards, using my right foot to trip her up, so that she fell towards the arm of the chair. I grabbed her under the waist with one hand and held onto her neck with the other. Then I pushed her down so that her face brushed the cushion and

I could manipulate her body so that her head and shoulders were under the far arm, her stomach resting on the near one, her rounded buttocks straining against the material of her dress.

"Please," she said, quietly. "Please, I will do whatever you want. You're right about me; I do know how to please a man. Let me up and I'll show you."

She tried to reach behind her, obviously aiming to take my balls in her hand, but my mood was far from charitable that day.

"Listen, darling," I told her. "I know that you will please me after I have given you a taste of my belt. I absolutely guarantee that you will perform to my entire satisfaction. And if you don't, then you can feel its kiss again – understand?"

Without waiting for a reply I lifted Lupita's dress and left it resting against the small of her back. She was wearing tights – a hideous garment cursed by God I am sure – and I didn't waste a second in pulling the nylon down to the owner's knees. Lupita's bottom was now only protected by thin pink cotton panties. I paused for a moment to admire the view as I had to admit that for a forty-odd year old Mexican, Lupita didn't look all that bad, but duty called as it always does and I peeled the final layer of protection down and left them hanging pathetically just above the tights.

She began to move, not violently, but she did wiggle her hips to try and keep her buttocks in motion, obviously thinking that a moving target would be harder to hit. Stupid woman – all it did was make her look more desirable and leave me wondering how she would move when the belt had really livened her up?

"Right, madam," I told her. You're going to get twelve, it's going to hurt, and you're going to wish that you had not raised your hand to me long before it's over." Crack! I brought the folded black leather down across her helpless, upturned buttocks. Crack! I brought it down again.

Lupita's gyrations had become quite intense, but she had not uttered a sound up to that moment. I wondered how long her stoicism would last when the leather really began to bite? Crack! Bite it did for the third time, and with all the strength of my arm behind it.

That was enough for Lupita. She turned to look at me as best she could, given her position with her head trapped under the arm of a chair, and I saw the liquid glow of tears forming in her eyes. Crack! The belt wrapped itself across her buttocks once again. Crack! I let fly with another stinger, and Luipta tried to raise her head, failed and let out a long low moan.

"Please, have pity," she said. Crack! The pity was all used up that day, as I stepped back to admire my handiwork with the chastisement half way to its completion. Lupita's buttocks were now a bright red, with an admittedly brighter glow on the right cheek. I moved around to the other side so that I could even up the colouration with the remaining strokes.

Crack! The belt came down a seventh time and Lupita broke down in tears with the sheer emotion of it all. You really would have needed a heart of stone not to laugh, but luckily I have one and I brought the belt down through a great swishing arc to crash against the bright red buttocks that lay at the end of the journey. Crack!

Crack! Crack! Crack! I laid on three in quick succession, as Lupita began to howl and kick her legs in a futile attempt to avoid the retribution that was not over yet.

Crack! The penultimate stroke hit home, but Lupita was too far gone to care that she only had one more cut to endure. She was now close to hysteria and sobbed with great gulping gasps as she fought to take air into her lungs.

I paused for a moment, long enough for Lupita to think that her punishment was over. Nobody said a word and the only sound in the room was the wretched woman's sobs.

"One more to go," I told her.

"Noooooooo!"

Crack! The belt hit its target for the twelfth and final time. Lupita's buttocks were a fiery red and I was pleased to see that both buttocks were now of a similar colour. I doubted that Lupita would thank me for my efforts; in fact I doubted that she was going to be in a position to do anything for quite some time as her sobs had a touch of hysteria about them.

Which was a pity as the fucking was about to commence...

I suppose at this point you are expecting to be told that I dragged Lupita to the bed and riveted her so rigid that she couldn't walk properly afterwards. Sorry, folks, but it is not my style to drag anyone anywhere. Lupita was going to do as she was told because all her options had been closed off, so I left her blubbering, took off my clothes, and then climbed into bed and lit a cigarette.

"Are you planning to cry all day, because this cock needs attention?" I remarked as I ground the remains of my cigarette out on an ashtray. To show that I was serious I threw back the bed covers so that Lupita could see my blue veiner, which though I say it myself was in a fine cervix tickling form that afternoon.

When Lupita looked up there was a strange expression on her face as if she had made a decision. She ceased her theatrics and began to undress herself without uttering a word or looking in my direction. She had that same look of determination on her face as she climbed into bed and without so much as a by your leave took my throbbing hardness in her hand.

"Now then," she said, very quietly and without once batting an eyelid. "I am going to show you what a Durango whore can do."

So she was from Durango, was she? That made sense since Durango is an arid lump of northern desert that is good only for cacti, thieves and tarts such as Lupita.

Give the girl credit she did show me what a Durango whore could do, and what she did she did incredibly well. I had tried to sit up as she climbed into bed but she pushed me onto my back and then straddled me as if I was a stallion that she was about to ride. Which I suppose in a way I was...

"I hate those things," I told her as I spied the condom that she had seemingly conjured up from nowhere. "It's like having a bath with my socks on."

Lupita didn't say anything; she just bit her lower lip and started to fondle a breast with one hand. Then she started to thrust her pelvis backwards and forwards, groaning softly all the while as she did it. Once she had my undivided attention, which didn't take long let's be honest, she bent forward to take my hardness in her mouth – and before I knew what was happening the condom had been fitted nice and snugly over my cock! That's right; she had somehow placed it in her own mouth and then fitted it over me as she deep throated my cock. Only Lupita and Marina, the girl that I introduced you to in the previous chapter have ever done that trick on me and it is still the only way that I will allow my chopper to go out with an overcoat on.

Having got me kitted out; Lupita then climbed aboard and immediately took my sword all the way up to its hilt. In spite of her years she was still tight inside, and I slid into her warm wetness with ease. She used her muscles to hold me once I was inside her and placed her hands on my shoulders to hold me down. I tried to push backwards against the mattress so that I could get some room to allow my cock to drive into her again, but as I pulled back she pushed down so remained embedded in her, unable to move. To be honest the tables had been well and truly turned.

"What's the matter, güero?" she asked, using the Mexican word for a white man.

I laughed and tried to use my strength to push her back, but she had ridden many a man before me and knew how to use her position to overcome my superior strength. Whether I liked it or not, Lupita was in control.

She lifted herself up slightly so that only the tip of my cock was inside her lips. Every time I tried to push further in she pulled away, slowly grinding herself in circles to keep my cock hard but not allowing me to shaft her properly. I felt the frustration build up inside me and so did Lupita as she began to let me push inside her a little more, but maddeningly not enough to really give her the fucking that I wanted to give. She had a grin on her face because she knew exactly the effect that she was having on me as she built up the pressure in my balls until they began to feel dull and heavy, aching for their release.

I somehow managed to push her hands away from my body and then I could put my hands underneath her and lift her body away from mine. I literally lifted her off me and for a few seconds held her up and over me before I dumped her to one side. Then I put Lupita on her back and climbed aboard her for the final ride home.

"So you are a man, after all, are you" she mocked. "Finally figured out how to fuck a woman... Yes, yes, give it to me, harder, harder than that. Make me scream, güero, make me scream."

So I did. I drove into as hard and fast as I could, and every time I pushed my cock into her slick wetness she clenched her muscles so that I had to drive past them and that excited me still further. I felt my balls filling, getting ready to empty, and that, of course, was exactly what this expert whore wanted.

"I am coming! I am coming!" I cried out as I felt my release happening.

Within seconds of our bout ending Lupita had climbed out of bed, and within five minutes she was showered and dressed, all ready to leave.

"You will keep your promise," she said. It was a statement, not a question.

I nodded and gave my word that I would. I did too, and Pedro got his loan I'm pleased to say.

"Why were you such a prime bitch earlier?" I asked her.

"I thought all that was behind me," she said with a shrug.

"El que no transa no avanza," I reminded her. In Spanish the words rhyme perfectly and mean that if you don't hustle you don't get anywhere. Only a fool is honest, and Mexicans may be many things but stupid they are not.

Lupita nodded at the truism and picked up her bag.

"Call me if you fancy a repeat performance," I said to her back as she walked to the door. She didn't answer; she just raised her arm in a farewell salute and without looking back at me once, opened the door, walked through it and closed it behind her.

Needless to say I never saw her again.

I suppose that you are wondering about Molly aren't you? Well, a couple of months later she got in touch, seeking out a favour. She was at a university where I had connections and had managed to fail some of her exams that semester. Luckily, I knew one of her tutors, so it was a simple matter to call him and sort matters out in the traditional back-scratching way. He was only too pleased to help since it put me in his debt and you never know when a friend might come in handy, do you?

Molly and I met one afternoon in the same hotel that I had used with her mother and I am pleased to report that Moll performed with all the genuine enthusiasm for the cock that her mother had so singularly lacked. That said, she didn't have one ounce of her mother's expertise at milking a bull pretty much to order: still she was a good rattle for all that.

We saw each other from time to time, usually when Molly needed something, and give her credit she never once tried to cheat me out of my payment.

You are wondering why I am not giving you a full report, I can tell. That's because I never spanked her – not once. I remember one day asking her why she was such a good girl. Her reply had me in fits of laughter:

"My mother couldn't sit down for a week after that day with you!"

So I never got to spank Molly, but it is nice that my strictures to a mother had been so well taken on board by her daughter.

Two Cuban Sisters

Cuba may be a long way from the United Kingdom, but Havana is a short hop of just over an hour from Mexico City and quite a few Mexicans nip over there for weekends. I was last there in 2005 which was when I not only had the pleasure of smacking two Cuban girls' bottoms, but I also discovered the sheer delight that mixing the lecture in with the spanking brings. Well, brings to me, I really can't say what the girls feel since I haven't actually asked any of them. Best not to, really, since they would probably moan vociferously and have to be spanked all over again for their sauce.

Havana had suffered hurricane damage shortly before I arrived and although she looked as lovely as ever, power blackouts were still the order of the day and night as the power grid was slowly repaired. I was staying at the hotel Nacional de Cuba and even that was running on backup power so I decided one evening after dark that a walk along the promenade was called for, and I left the hotel, walked down an incredibly steep, but thankfully short, street called la Rampa and crossed the main road to the promenade.

Havana is blessed with lots of places to sit and I chose a stone bench that was shaped like a horseshoe to sit down and have a cigarette. The back of the bench was about five feet high, obviously to shade the area during the day, but at night in a city without power it created a very private spot indeed. The sky was moonless that night and literally the only light was provided by my pocket torch. Having lit my cigarette I switched the torch off to save the battery and that was when my night's adventure began.

"Switch the light back on," cried a female voice from somewhere in front of me. She spoke with the accent of Cuba so was obviously not a tourist, and curious to see who was sharing the seats with me I flicked on my light.

Sitting about ten feet away on the other side of the horseshoe were two girls, both in their late teens or early twenties and both wearing thin cotton skirts and the usual garish T-shirts that all Latin-Americans seem to love so much.

"Want to join me?" I asked, waving the pair of them over. Both girls promptly scampered across to sit on either side of me.

"My name's Maria," said the slightly taller of the two who was sitting on my right. I liked the way my torch shone its light through her long black hair and made it seem translucent. I was also impressed by the way her heavy breasts moved of their own accord under her Dallas Cowboys shirt. Cuban women are noted throughout the region for their love of the bra-less look.

"I am Elena," chirped the voice to my left. Her twin girls were just as large as the pair carried by Maria, and equally free to roam beneath a T-shirt that advertised Joe's Body Shop in Ontario.

"Sisters?" I asked after inspecting both of them with the light.

"Yes," Elena sang, in her quite delicious voice.

"How old are you both?"

"I'm twenty," Maria replied for the two of them, "and Elena is eighteen."

"How nice... And what are your plans for the evening?"

"We don't have any," replied Maria. "Where are you taking us?"

The nice thing about speaking the local language is that you do not have to spend an arm and a leg in the tourist traps, so at my urging the girls took me to a quiet bar where we could sit and talk. Now it is true that quiet is a relative concept because no Latin bar can be truly quiet and the place was actually quite raucous, but at least they did not want to charge me in dollars for the local firewater that they served.

Both girls were students: Maria was about to enter the third year of her four year degree course at the University of Havana, and Elena was eagerly anticipating her entry to the university having just left school. The girls lived with their mother on the other side of town and the conversation ran far and wide as two bright eyed and seriously sexy girls giggled and flirted the evening away.

I danced with Elena who wrapped her arms around me and wanted to know if I liked her enough to go somewhere with her? Then Maria nibbled my ear and wondered the same thing. I put both girls minds at rest by telling them that I quite fancied the pair of 'em and where could we go so they could ride the cock horse?

The two girls looked at each other and proceeded to giggle some more. Then Maria told me that maybe it would be better another night because they had to get up early the next day to go shopping as they wanted to go and buy shoes, and would I like to take them, and…

I put a stop to this nonsense by offering them cold hard cash there and then. Frankly the thought of being dragged around the shops by one female is bad enough, but any man who agrees to go shopping with two is insane. I still think that I got the better of the deal.

As we left the bar little did any of us know that before the night was out both girls would be nursing very sore bottoms indeed, but that was in the future. Standing outside the bar with Elena on my arm as we waited for Maria to join us everything seemed wonderful.

Once Maria had joined us we climbed aboard a taxi and I sat back waiting for one of the girls to give directions to the driver. The problem was that neither of them spoke so there was kind of pregnant pause as the two girls looked at me, obviously expecting me to have some idea of where we might head.

"Where shall we go?" Maria asked, eventually, a look of utter helplessness in her eyes.

"Do I sound like a Cuban to you? I think I sound like someone from Mexico City who is here on holiday and doesn't have a clue where to go," I replied, trying to choke back my laughter. It still seemed funny at that point as I assumed that eventually one of the girls would think of something.

One of them did and we went off on a wild goose chase to a flat that a friend lived in, but he had gone out for the evening. The taxi driver said that he had a cousin who might help so we set off in the direction of God knew where, but the cousin was entertaining a lady and needed the bed for himself and her.

Finally the girls came up with a third address and this time the occupant, who was yet another cousin, was not only at home, but he was alone and more than happy to take some money off me to vacate his property for an hour or two. If this sounds incredible then we are talking about Latin-America here and the whole region works on mores of its own, but Cuba adds an extra layer of incredibleness to the pot. Basically, people will quite happily hand over their whole flat to a working girl with whom they have an arrangement. She enters with her client and the family go and sit outside for the duration of the bout.

So we went into the flat, still with only my torch to give us any light. One of the girls spied a candle in a saucer and that was lit to illuminate out way to the bedroom. Once there we went through the giggly performance of stripping the two sisters down to their luscious flesh, then they pulled off my clothing and we all climbed into bed.

"Where are your condoms?" asked Maria.

"Don't have any," I replied, taking a bouncer in each hand and sticking my head between them. As you know, I just love doing that to big, melon like tits and then saying "brrrrr."

"Wait," announced Maria. "I'll go and get some."

"No you bloody well won't," I told her. "This hard-on doesn't need a coat."

Instead of taking hold of the proffered member like a good little girl should, Maria scampered out of bed, threw her clothes on and was trotting off in the direction of the door before I fully realised what was happening. I turned to Elena with a shrug, but she was throwing clothes on and then she charged after her sister leaving me and my blue-veiner alone in a strange flat. Feeling somewhat put out I settled down to wait their return, and decided at the moment that two little girls' bottoms were going to tingle at the very least.

I doubt if I had been alone for more than a minute when I heard a commotion just outside the front door. I could hear what sounded like Maria's voice protesting about something or other so I pulled my clothes on and went to investigate. I saw a gaggle of policemen pushing Elena into a car, Maria being told to take her hook or they would nick her as well, and then a cop turned to look at me and I just knew that it was going to be one of those nights.

In Cuba if the cops take an interest in you then they are not looking for a bribe, unlike the rest of their Latin-American brethren. Cuba's police not only look as if they know the value of soap and water, but they carry themselves with a dignity and pride that does their country proud in the abstract, but doesn't actually help people from the rest of the region sort out their little problems in the time honoured way. This encounter was going to need careful handling, I decided.

Choosing the most senior looking officer I shook his hand as one always does and introduced myself, making damn sure that I also told him that I was from Mexico, just in case my funny sounding name led him to believe that I was a wicked American.

"Tell me, comrade officer, how may I be of service to you?" I enquired in my plummiest tones. I tell you, when it comes to large black Cuban men with big Russian guns on their hips, then I can grovel with the best of 'em.

"The matter does not concern you, comrade, er, whatever your name is," said the head cop, as he tried to make out the name on the Mexican driving license that I had thought politic to show him as identification.

"I am pleased to hear that," I said with real feeling. "But tell me what the problem is and maybe we can resolve it." No fool me; I know that the Cubans use the verb To Resolve whenever they plan to do something not exactly legal.

The cop pursed his lips and I could see his mind working overtime. How far could he trust me? In his mind I was Mexican so that meant I was used to paying off the police, but could I be some kind of undercover operative brought in to keep his crew on their toes? All this and more went through that man's mind in an instant. His eyes narrowed and he stared at me intently.

We then began a sophisticated linguistic dance where neither of us gave anything away, and from which both of us could deny the reality of the conversation if we had to. Eventually we both dried up, because neither of us could find the exact words to get to the bottom of the matter.

What exactly do you want, comrade? asked the cop, eventually.

I threw caution to the wind. Why bother anymore? Time to tell the truth:

"These two little darlings are due to attend to my cock," I told the assembled throng. "And the cock badly needs the attention!"

The cops just burst out laughing. I couldn't believe it but all the tension went out of the air and we were just a group of men stood around killing time with our talk.

"What do you want with these two?" I asked the cops.

"That one," said the head man, indicating Elena, "is out without her identity card."

I knew enough about Cuba to know that this is a serious matter. I looked around at my new friends and decided that the Mexican approach just might work.

"If you let her go then your wives will be pleased at the presents you can afford to buy them," I said, before getting the next surprise of the night when the cops refused point blank to take a penny off me. Not only that, but they decided to take Elena to her house where she would show them her document and then they would return her to me!

Maria was gently pushed over in my direction and the cops started to leave with Elena in hand. Turning around just before he got into his patrol car the head man put his cigarette in his mouth, and considered both me an Marina in turn

"She has a big mouth," he told me with a grin. Then, incredibly, he held his right arm outstretched with the palm held facing up. He wasn't after a handout; No, he waved the hand from side to side in a time-honoured Latin way. For the benefit of my Saxon readers the gesture is an invitation to spank, something which Maria understood only too well.

"Nooo," she wailed, and made to take off. I grabbed her by the arm and started to drag her into the house, with the raucous laughter of the cops ringing in my ears.

"Thank you, officers," I said, as I pulled Maria into the house and closed the door behind us.

"Right young lady," I told her. "You are now in more trouble than you know!"

"What have I done?" Maria wailed with the eternal cry of the female who knows that retribution is heading her way at a rate of knots, but hopes to avoid the inevitable with a succession of silly questions.

I put a stop to this old nonsense by grabbing the girl firmly by the shoulders and giving her a good shake. Then I pushed her against a wall and spoke quietly into her ear, annunciating every word with extra care:

"Now you listen to me, madam. If you are going to pick fellows up on the street then you had better have a stack of condoms handy, otherwise be prepared to be ridden bareback. Do I look as if I get pregnant? Don't you think that a whore going out without a condom is like a carpenter without a saw? It's a tool of your fucking trade!"

"I'm not a whore," Maria wailed.

"Yeah? What do you call a girl who takes money for sex? Mother fucking Teresa?"

"I only do it when I want something," Maria whimpered. Clearly her desperation to avoid the spanking that was now just seconds away had interfered with her ability to reason logically – although who can tell where women are concerned?

In any event I was in no mood to listen to any more prattle so I put a stop to further debate by spinning the wretched girl around and encircling her waist with my right arm. Then I picked her up to leave her body dangling against my right hip. Leaning slightly to the left so as to hold her in that helpless position I walked purposefully over to a sofa that sat in the middle of the room.

I dropped her to her feet and before she had time to figure out her next move I promptly sat down and yanked her across my left thigh. Before Maria had time to even open her mouth my right leg was cocked over her thighs and both her wrists were held in left hand. With the other hand I flipped up her skirt to reveal a firm, pair of golden olive buttocks, clad only in a black thong. I paused for a moment to consider the admittedly rather pleasing view, and then I hooked my fingers into the elastic of her scanties and started to peel them down.

"Noooooo"! Maria started to howl and kicked her legs like a wild horse. She turned her head to the left to look at me imploringly: "Noooooo! Nooooo! Not on the bare, please, please not on the bare," she pleaded.

"Don't be silly," I told her, letting go of her panties and giving her rump a firm smack. "You are wearing a thong – it leaves your bottom bare as it is!

Yes, yes, it does," said the increasingly anxious girl.

"It gives you no protection at all, does it?

"No it doesn't," Maria agreed, shaking her head frantically.

"Fine, so it doesn't matter if I pull it down then," and pull the thong down I promptly did, to the accompaniment of a howl that was ear shattering in its decibel level.

The spanking began with a succession of solid smacks on alternate cheeks of Maria's upturned rump that left her bottom a bright red. She clenched the cheeks to try and reduce the size of the target and ludicrously pressed her stomach into my leg as if the extra inch or so of space that she gained would somehow serve to shield her defenceless buttocks from my hard male palm.

As the spanking progressed Maria twisted her upper body so she could turn her face towards me, obviously feeling that if I could see the look of anguish on her face then I would take pity on her plight. As each smack cracked across her bare bottom she winced, and bit her lower lip, her eyes rapidly filling with tears.

"Please, please tell me what I have done," she blubbered eventually, with a question so ludicrous that it made me pause my labours for a moment whilst I considered my reply.

"Do you want the whole list or just the main three or four reasons? I asked. How about your failure to even have a room prepared for us to go to? Do you think that I enjoyed the guided tour of Havana by night?

Without waiting for a reply I began to spank her again, and for some reason I gave Maria twenty-five smacks, each one bouncing over her bottom to leave the imprint of my hand firmly engraved on the cheeks of her helpless bottom. Maria wailed like a banshee as the correction continued on its remorseless course, wriggling her bottom with an unconscious lasciviousness, in a desperate attempt to avoid her well merited spanking.

Again I stopped and rested a moment before speaking to the helpless girl again:

Are you planning to forget your condoms again?

I started the spanking again, and again I landed twenty-five smacks to that upturned bottom. I laid on those smacks with all the force of my arm behind them, and Maria threw back her head and howled in impotent helplessness, her feet drumming a constant tattoo on the floor as she tried to break free from my iron grip.

"Planning to go running off again? That's why the damned cops got involved in all this, isn't it? You and Elena in the street!"

Once again I began to smack Maria's poor, swollen and very red bottom. As with the previous sessions I administered twenty-five smacks, first to one cheek and then the other, as the by then well chastised girl sobbed the tears of bitter repentance, but still managed to find the spirit to continue her futile attempts to break free and end the discipline.

"Do you want me to go on?" I asked, rhetorically.

"Nooooo! Nooooo! Nooooo! Please, please stop, wailed Maria, and all of a sudden her struggle ceased and she lay, totally conquered and completely unable to mount any further resistance across my knee. To prove the point I released her wrists from my grip, and unhooked my leg from its position atop her no longer scissoring thighs. Then I smacked her bottom again. Hard, solid smacks which Maria could have avoided just by climbing of my knee, but she didn't as I knew she wouldn't. She just lay there, her body twitching with each smack, waiting obediently like a good girl should for her ordeal to end.

The spanking was over, I decided, as I sat back and let Maria sob her heart out across my knee. She lay there in a state of total submission and made no attempt to rise. Eventually, I lifted her up and placed her head on my shoulder. Instinctively she wrapped her arms around my neck and sobbed her heart out, her tears splashing on my cheek.

Suddenly I heard a noise to my right. Turning to see what it was I saw that the door was open – I must have left it on the latch, but I was sure that I had closed it – and two of the cops were stood in the doorway with big grins on her faces. Stood between them was Elena who wasn't grinning at all. In fact she looked decidedly unhappy as I let Maria fall gently to the floor and went to take charge of her younger, but equally guilty, sister.

Elena was visibly shaking as I strolled over to her. In fact if it hadn't been for the two cops who stood on either side of her I suspect that she would have collapsed in a heap on the floor. To be honest I find the sight of any woman in that state thoroughly agreeable, but this was made doubly so by the fact that Elena's stupidity in leaving her identification card at home had pretty much created the night's nonsense. On the subject of the card, I asked the cops what had happened.

"She left it at home, just as she said," explained the senior of the two plods, fishing in his breast pocket for a cigar. A Romeo y Julieta I noticed, and I nodded to him as a salute of his fine taste.

"In her other handbag," explained the second policeman. "She changed her clothes at the last minute and the other handbag did not match to colour of," he waved his hand rather than finish the sentence and I sighed my understanding. Wherever you go in the world the story is always the same: females and their superficialities never cease to amaze me.

"I hope that I didn't keep you waiting," I told the two men. "As you will have seen I was rather busy so didn't notice you."

"Not to worry," said cigar man, wreathing the room in the warm, pungent, masculine aroma of that greatest of all cigars.

Elena began to cough, obviously in an attempt to curry favour.

"There is something you wish to say?" I asked her.

"No," she replied.

"Good keep it that way," I told her. "Comrade Officers," I continued, addressing the two men. How can I thank you.

"Nothing needs to be said, the matter is closed," cigar man said.

"Please, won't you at least take something for your troubles?"

The two cops looked at each other and then looked at me without replying. I fished into my wallet and gave them 500 Mexican pesos which is about £25 and about double what I would have given the Mexican police for a similar service, but I was feeling generous and relieved that everything was going to turn out well.

Turn out well for me, that is. I doubt if Elena was sharing my hail fellow well met attitude as I showed my two guests out of the building, in fact I know that she wasn't because as I closed to door I saw that she was leaning against the wall with her hand over her mouth staring in rapt attention at Maria who was still on the floor where I had left her. Actually, she was staring at Maria's bottom, the silly girl having failed to cover herself following her session across my knee. Obviously Maria was a bit of an exhibitionist I decided as I walked up behind Elena and grabbed her by the arm.

Her head shot up and she turned to look at me with a pair of wide, staring eyes that literally oozed the fear that lay behind them. She tried to smile but it came out as almost a grimace and from deep within her, almost at the level of her soul, there emerged a long, low moan.

My smile was that of a man perfectly at ease with himself and the world...

"Have you any idea how hard I am going to smack your bottom?" I asked in what I thought were genial tones.

Elena shook her head frantically. Clearly she had no idea so it was going to fall to me to show her just how hard the spanking was going to be. I mentioned this to her and she placed both hands on my chest and looked at me imploringly.

"I have my identity document with me," she said, as if that would excuse everything.

I didn't waste my breath replying. I just hauled her towards the sofa that I had sat on to chastise Maria and when we reached it I stopped, grabbed her by the chin and then turned her face up to mine.

"Now then, little girl," I said. It is time to find out just how hard I can smack your bottom, isn't it?"

Elena started to dance from one foot to the other, biting her lower lip as she did so. Then she grabbed the collar of my polo shirt and with her thumbs inside the opening she ran her hands up and down, looking at my appealingly all the while.

"Please, please," was all she said as her dance became more and more pronounced.

I looked into her eyes and grabbed her by the shoulders intending to give her a similar shake to the one that I had given to Maria. As I did so she put her face into her hands and then buried her head in my chest. She stopped her little dance and I heard a noise like water trickling through a tap onto a stone sink and I knew at once what was happening. Elena had lost control of her bladder and was wetting herself and the floor. Her sobs took on a note of hysteria as she threw back her head and wept the bitter tears of total humiliation.

Holding Elena tightly by the arms I stood there with her, waiting until the sobs had subsided a little, which would indicate that the hysteria had passed, something which did not take long to happen.

"I am going to smack your bare bottom until it is the colour of a ripe tomato," I then told her, without any drama and in a quiet voice.

For a moment I thought that Elena was going to resist with the same intent that Maria had demonstrated, but then her head fell forward onto my chest and her shoulders slumped. This naughty girl was not going to give any trouble at all.

I sat down on the sofa and pulled Elena over my knee. Making sure that her skirt did not ride up at the front so that I could keep my trousers dry, I carefully lifted her short skirt to reveal a firm bottom clad in white cotton bikini panties. That sodden garment I slowly peeled down to leave the scanties hanging around her knees. During this whole period as I prepared Elena for her correction she neither moved not made a sound, she just lay there quietly as if accepting that her behaviour had brought her to this shameful state.

Once I had bared the wretched girl's bottom I raised my right hand high above my head and without further ado brought it crashing down upon those golden orbs. I spanked her methodically and soundly, laying on the palm to fist one cheek and then the other. Elena's bottom quickly began to turn a bright red under my hand's ministrations and her buttock cheeks twitched unconsciously, but throughout the correction she did not even attempt to cover her bottom, she just lay quietly as her chastisement continued.

As will Maria I paused the spanking after twenty-five smacks or so and addressed the girl as she lay across my knee:

"Forget your documents, will you? Look what happens when you do!"

My hand cracked down across her bare bottom again and again, each smack sounding like a gunshot in the close confines of the room. The second tranche of smacks was identical to the first, with each crack of the hand well laid on, alternating the cheeks, slowly but surely covering the whole bottom with my hand, leaving not an inch that had not felt the painful smack of my hard hand as I taught the silly girl not to break her own country's basic rules and regulations.

Finally I brought the spanking to a close and sat back to admire my handiwork. I had not spanked Elena half as hard as I had disciplined Maria, but to be fair she was younger and had not put up anything like the struggle that Maria had attempted. Let that be a lesson to all you naughty chits who might be reading this: put up a fight and your spanking is likely to be twice as long and three times as hard as it might otherwise have been. Not that they will take heed from my words – women never learn do they?

I dumped Elena onto the floor where she lay next to her sister and partner in crime. The two culprits sat with their legs underneath them so that their ravished bottoms were not in contact with the hard concrete floor. They leaned against each other for comfort and apart from the sobbing that came from two suitably corrected females there was no noise in the room. At least there wasn't until I opened my mouth and addressed both of them:

"Right girls – who is first to be fucked?"

Maria climbed to her feet, and then helped the still distraught Elena to rise. Both girls looked up at me piteously, Maria holding her sorely tried bottom as Elena tried to organise her skirt so that it did not get too wet from her little accident as it were. I decided that Elena really needed to be told what to do, and whilst she was doing it I would entertain myself with Maria.

"Elena," I told her. "Go and find the bathroom and have a nice long shower. Then wash your clothes and leave them to dry while you are with us in the bedroom." I paused at looked at her ripe, melon-like boobs. "Better make it a quick shower," I concluded.

Maria was next and I turned to give her the order that would take us to the bedroom, but before I could open my mouth she had given her sister a final glance and turning on her heel she began to walk stiff-legged to the bedroom, still holding her bottom gingerly.

We reached the door of what I assumed was the bedroom and Maria opened it. Yes, that was a bedroom, as there was a double bed, and as Maria entered the room I gave her a firm but friendly pat to the rear to encourage her along.

"Nooooo," she yelped, obviously feeling that further ministrations on my part were not needed. What can you do with women, eh? I was only trying to be friendly.

Standing by the side of the bed I was expecting Maria to try and dissuade me from mounting her, but she surprised me by quickly shuffling off her clothes, and then stood in front of me in all her magnificence, hands behind her back, her chest trust out so that I could admire her fine bouncers. She had the most delightful smile on her face, and she cocked her head to one side as women often do, before pouting prettily at me.

"You have a heavy hand," she said, increasing the pout level substantially.

She smiled a trifle ruefully I thought and then surprised me again by pulling my polo shirt over my head and tossing it to the floor. Then she slowly unzipped my jeans and reached inside, brushing her hand through the opening in my boxer shorts to take my throbbing hardness in her hand. Her smile widened as she felt it grow in her hand.

"It's big," she said quietly, a thickness coming to her voice.

Maria unbuttoned the jeans and then pushed them down over my hips so that they fell around my ankles. I sat down to remove my sandals and the denim, and as I did so Maria knelt in front of me and without any fuss took my cock in her mouth. For the next few minutes the only sounds in the room came from her mouth as she sucked my hardness and my groans of pleasure as she did so.

Eventually I stopped her and stepped out of my shorts. Then I signalled her to climb into bed. Maria got to her feet, but instead of getting straight into bed she wrapped her arms around my neck and whispered a plea in my ear to be gentle.

"Of course I will," I told her. You're a good girl now, aren't you?"

Maria nodded her head and then got into bed, wincing as the mattress touched her freshly spanked bottom. She gingerly turned to lie on her side, something which made me smile slightly to watch. That smile turned into a huge grin as I saw that Elena was coming into the bedroom. She was as naked as her sister, her wet clothes in one hand. Deftly she placed them over a chair and then without a murmur she got into the bed to lie next to her older sister.

There was nothing else for it but to climb in between them. Looking at our respective skin colours I felt like the cheese in a lightly toasted sandwich. I said something about it to the girls and it made them both giggle deliciously.

I was on my back and I took the girls' necks in each of my hands and first one then the other, I brought them over to kiss me, each kiss long and slow and lingering. When I was kissing Maria, for perhaps the second or third time, Elena leaned over and took my cock in her mouth. I thought at that moment that I had left the earth behind and entered the gates of paradise.

Maria began to squirm, at first I thought that it was the mattress touching her bottom again, but then I realised that it was pure arousal that made her move her hips like that and open her mouth in almost a snarl. I reached down to touch between her thighs and was delighted to feel her slick, warm wetness. This girl was ready; I resolved to take her first.

I turned Maria onto her stomach and placed a pillow under her tummy. Then I climbed between her thighs from the rear and mounted her. My cock slid smoothly into her wetness, and as I pushed it slowly home, she exhaled deeply in time with the thrust.

Slowly, because there was no need to hurry at all, I thrust in and out of Maria's tight warm body, slow and steady strokes, and my cock moving with the same remorseless intent as the piston on a steam engine. Then, I pulled my cock out until just the uppermost tip was between her lips and waited, waited as she wriggled her hips to try to take more of it.

"Please," she said, laughing at her own plight, and I drove my cock home, firmly up to the hilt. Then I repeated the procedure and Maria began to pant more and more, her hips rising to meet each thrust, her red, well-spanked buttocks pressing lewdly into my stomach as I drove into her, harder and harder, faster and faster.

Maria began to pant heavily; a scream built up inside her throat and then escaped to bounce off the walls with a deafening intensity. She took one of my hands and put the knuckle into her mouth, her hips moving at a frantic rate, and then she sunk her teeth into the knuckle, biting so hard that I thought she must have drawn blood as she reached her moment of ecstasy.

I collapsed on top of her and planned to rest for a while, but I felt Elena's hand on my back and turned my head to look at her. She was lying on her side, watching us intently between hooded eyes, one hand on a breast, idly stroking her nipple, keeping it hard and firm. I climbed off Maria's back and as I did so Elena rolled over onto her back and opened her thighs to receive me. As I climbed between her legs she reached down and took my hardness in her hand, guiding it into her body with a practised ease.

She may only have been 18 but Elena knew how to milk a bull! As I drove into her body she thrust her hips up in time with my drives, squeezing her inner muscles as tightly as she could as each stroke went home, and her nails raking my back so deeply that she drew blood.

"Fuck me! Fuck me harder! Harder!" Elena urged me on to pleasure her with greater vigour and I increased the speed and intensity of my thrust in response to her demands.

I felt my balls filling, becoming heavier, and I thrust into her body, the sweat dripping from my face, my cock hard and powerful, pushing into her body time and time and time again. Elena reached behind me and I felt her fingers probe my rear, and then incredibly she pushed her middle finger into my rectum, holding it there with the tip inside me, circling it around and around, and opening my body. I tried to clench the muscles but her finger was stronger, and I at that moment my balls could no longer hold their hot liquid and I spilled my seed into her, both of us crying out at the final moment.

The three of us lay in a heap, all sated by our experience. I was stunned by the difference between the two sisters; Maria had behaved pretty much as I expected a newly disciplined girl to act, but Elena had been a delightful surprise. I must be honest and say that I have never known a female like her, every other girl or woman that I have been forced to discipline has behaved like Maria: Elena was and is totally unique in her response.

Time marched on and we all went to shower together and then after getting dressed we left the house and returned it to its rightful owner. That man was sat patiently outside chatting to a neighbour and looked quite relieved that we were leaving. Although it has to be said that he was quite happy to take delivery of a handful of Mexican notes, and told me that I was welcome any time – so long as I brought my wallet, presumably.

I saw the girls again over the following week, but there was no need to spank either of them again as both were obedient with none of the provocations that had led to such sore bottoms on the night that we had met. I made love to Elena on the Havana promenade one night during yet another blackout, and Maria took my cock in her mouth in the back of a taxi the following evening, but when I think of those two charmers I think of the night when I took two Cuban sisters and spanked the naughtiness out of them before fucking them both until we were all so exhausted that we could barely walk afterwards.

From mothers and daughters to a couple of Cuban sisters via any number of other lovely girls who came in a variety of skin tones from light olive to dusky red – I spanked and poked any number of them during my years in Mexico. They behaved like their sisters had in Britain, with squeals of protest as their dignity was stripped from them along with their knickers.

And it isn't over yet!

ENDPIECE

Looking back down the decades from 1971 to the present day in April 2011, I can say with total honesty that it has been a spanking good life.

My story does not end here, but it does reach a plateau where it must pause for a while. I went in hospital in early 2009 for a routine operation that went horribly wrong. Three months later, I emerged from a coma and it took me all that remained of the year to slowly recover some of my strength.

In the December I made my way painfully back to England and lived on the charity of friends for the first six months of 2010. Only as that year drew to a close did I start to regain my old form and slowly start to cast around for a way and a means with which to spend the rest of my life. This book is part of my attempt to start doing just that.

Writing this book allowed me to wander the highways of my mind and revisit crevices that I had either simply forgotten about or which lay buried deep in that spot in the back of the mind that is best left unexplored. Still, and for all that, the past forty years have now come together to make me the man that I am today, and I have picked out the most important highlights to present to you in the volume that you have just read.

Looking back down those long years, I am struck by the realisation of just how normal domestic spankings were when I was young. I am not suggesting that women and girls enthusiastically embraced the idea of having their bottoms smacked, but they did seem to accept that there were certain rules and if they were broken then bottoms would tingle. Growing up in that culture, I accepted the notion that one day I would smack a girl's bottom as being perfectly natural and when I finally did, the act of putting Anita across my knee just reinforced that viewpoint. The affairs that followed only served to entrench further that attitude in my mind, and had I not had the crisis in my personal life of 1980-81 I probably would not have even paused to wonder at that order, so natural did it seem to me.

Standing on the bridge that New Year's Day in 1982 I could have taken the easy option and just shrugged my shoulders and got on with life. A job would have turned up eventually and I suppose that I would have married someone or other, had children, and joined the darts team in a local pub. Instead, I decided to follow the Sinatra Option, as it were, and do things my way.

My way involved going to university and then on to a life abroad and in all of that time I was honest both to myself and to the women that I met. The last woman that I was faithful to was Helen in 1981 and that mistake will never be made again. However, I always tell a woman that if she wants faithfulness from a male then she might be better advised getting herself a nice little doggie than look for it in me. You may hate me for my cynicism but I hope that I have earned your respect for my honesty.

Another decision, taken on that bridge all those years ago has also stood me in good stead down the years. That was never to allow any woman to get so close to me that she could step on my heart. I am not a misogynist; I do not dislike women, but bless their conniving little hearts, as they are never again to be fully trusted by me.

Whether we are talking about Home Counties' girls at Oxford or the mixed bag that ranged from upper class creoles to American-Indians from Mexico, the rule has always been that when a woman gets out of line her bottom is smacked. If she objects to that then that really is the end of the affair. I do not regard spanking as part of role-play as I do not play such games. All the women that I have put over my knee have gone across it for some genuine reason, and it has been to teach them a lesson. The fact that on many occasions the lesson has to be relearned is neither here nor there, the principle stands that a good smacked bottom is as much a part of normal male female relations as the sex which invariably follows a spanking. In a nutshell, this is all about control, about maintaining that control, and about who wears the trousers in a relationship. The spanking is the first part – the sex is the second – and they are inherently connected.

There is one woman who understands these both intellectually and emotionally and I shall call her Raven. She is an executive who flounces around giving orders to men in suits, all of whom suffer periodic bouts of impotency at the mere mention of her name. If only they knew that on her London trips, the reason why she tends to wriggle in her seat is that I have soundly smacked her backside.

I was chatting on the telephone to the lady, and she told me about a married friend of hers in the UK who wished to meet a disciplinarian with a view to having her behaviour corrected as and when needed, but who would not take advantage of her après-spank state to give her a jolly good riveting. Needless to say, I fell about laughing at the sheer lunacy of such an idea.

"What kind of man would travel half way across the country to put a young chit in her place and then not give her a seeing to afterwards? I mean the whole point of a spanking is to reduce an insolent madam to the level of the obedient little girl. There is nothing finer," I concluded, and although I say it myself I was in fine fettle that night, "than to have a freshly spanked female. She is usually so keen to obey, that I find the sight rather touching."

"Yes, and that's why," began Raven, but I was in no mood to be interrupted by her female desire to prattle.

"And another thing," my voice boomed out, "what kind of woman would really expect such a man to even exist?"

Of course in May of 2010 I did come across one such female, but once I realised what her power kick was my anger was such that she did a runner, and quite rightly so. The idea that I would play the role of strict uncle without going on to exercise my middle leg is just too risible for words but that was what the silly cow wanted. However, most normal females are looking for a man who will bring them to heel, and that involves the bedroom as well. Otherwise, what is the point of it all?

"More pertinently," I went on, warming to my theme, "what would I get out of the deal, other than a sore hand and a banging great hard-on?"

"Absolutely," replied Raven. "And that is why I never thought of asking you to be her disciplinarian," she concluded, in hemlock sweet tones.

That is bloody women for you all over, and that is why my spanking good life must continue into the future. Damned women: they never learn do they?

Now come here, young lady: you know that you deserve this!
February – May 2011

ABOUT THE AUTHOR

Nick Urzdown is the pen name of a bon viveur and libertine, who has been writing on and off for many years. In real life, Nick is a graduate of Ruskin College, Oxford, the University of Manchester and a rather scratty polytechnic in South London. He went on to become the professor of North American History at a Mexican university and has a penis with a mind of its own which led him astray on more than one occasion with nubile young Mexican undergraduates. Ill health forced him to return to the United Kingdom in December 2009 and he now lives in Northern England. It amuses him to see the look of puzzlement on British people's faces when he tells them that the youngest two of his three sons were born six months apart. Mexicans understand immediately what happened, and he has resolved to spend the rest of his life trying to ensure that the British cease being quite so bovine. He blogs at strictuncle.blogspot.com.

Made in the USA
Columbia, SC
18 November 2017